GO!
with Microsoft®

Outlook 2016
Getting Started

Shelley Gaskin and Joan Lambert

330 Hudson Street, NY, NY 10013

M000294216

Vice President, Career Skills: Andrew Gilfillan
Executive Editor: Jenifer Niles
Team Lead, Project Management: Laura Burgess
Development Editor: Nancy Lamm
Editorial Assistant: Michael Campbell
Director of Product Marketing: Maggie Waples
Director of Field Marketing: Leigh Ann Sims
Field Marketing Managers: Molly Schmidt and Joanna Conley
Marketing Coordinator: Susan Osterlitz
Operations Specialist: Diane Peirano
Senior Art Director: Diane Ernsberger

Cover Photos: GaudiLab, Rawpixel.com, Pressmaster, Eugenio Marongiu, Boggy, Gajus, Rocketclips, Inc.
Associate Director of Design: Blair Brown
Director of Media Development: Blaine Christine
Media Project Manager, Production: John Cassar
Full-Service Project Management: Amy Kopperude
Composition: iEnergizer Aptara®, Ltd.
Printer/Binder: LSC Communications Harrisonburg
Cover Printer: LSC Communications Harrisonburg
Text Font: Times LT Pro

Credits and acknowledgments borrowed from other sources and reproduced, with permission, in this textbook appear on the appropriate page within text. Microsoft and/or its respective suppliers make no representations about the suitability of the information contained in the documents and related graphics published as part of the services for any purpose. All such documents and related graphics are provided "as is" without warranty of any kind.

Microsoft and/or its respective suppliers make no representations about the suitability of the information contained in the documents and related graphics published as part of the services for any purpose. All such documents and related graphics are provided "as is" without warranty of any kind. Microsoft and/or its respective suppliers hereby disclaim all warranties and conditions with regard to this information, including all warranties and conditions of merchantability, whether express, implied or statutory, fitness for a particular purpose, title and non-infringement. In no event shall Microsoft and/or its respective suppliers be liable for any special, indirect or consequential damages or any damages whatsoever resulting from loss of use, data or profits, whether in an action of contract, negligence or other tortious action, arising out of or in connection with the use or performance of information available from the services. The documents and related graphics contained herein could include technical inaccuracies or typographical errors. Changes are periodically added to the information herein. Microsoft and/or its respective suppliers may make improvements and/or changes in the product(s) and/or the program(s) described herein at any time. Partial screen shots may be viewed in full within the software version specified.

The documents and related graphics contained herein could include technical inaccuracies or typographical errors. Changes are periodically added to the information herein. Microsoft and/or its respective suppliers may make improvements and/or changes in the product(s) and/or the program(s) described herein at any time. Partial screen shots may be viewed in full within the software version specified.

Microsoft® and Windows® are registered trademarks of the Microsoft Corporation in the U.S.A. and other countries. This book is not sponsored or endorsed by or affiliated with the Microsoft Corporation.

Cataloging-in-Publication data is on file with the Library of Congress

3 17

ISBN 10:   0-13-449707-4
ISBN 13: 978-0-13-449707-5

Contents

About the Authors

Shelley Gaskin, Series Editor, is a professor in the Business and Computer Technology Division at Pasadena City College in Pasadena, California. She holds a bachelor's degree in Business Administration from Robert Morris College (Pennsylvania), a master's degree in Business from Northern Illinois University, and a doctorate in Adult and Community Education from Ball State University (Indiana). Before joining Pasadena City College, she spent 12 years in the computer industry, where she was a systems analyst, sales representative, and director of Customer Education with Unisys Corporation. She also worked for Ernst & Young on the development of large systems applications for their clients. She has written and developed training materials for custom systems applications in both the public and private sector, and has also written and edited numerous computer application textbooks.

This book is dedicated to my students, who inspire me every day.

Joan Lambert, President and CEO of Online Training Solutions, Inc., is a Microsoft Certified Professional, Microsoft Office Specialist Master, Microsoft Certified Technology Specialist for Windows and Windows Server, and a Microsoft Certified Trainer. She is the author or coauthor of more than three dozen books about Windows and Office, video-based training courses for SharePoint and OneNote, Office for iPad, and three generations of Microsoft Office Specialist certification study guides.

This book is dedicated to my daughter Trinity, who is my iDevice expert, and to my father, Steve Lambert, both of whom give me unfailing support and inspiration.

GO! with Outlook 2016 is the right solution for you and your students in the modern, fast-moving, mobile environment. The GO! Series content focuses on the real-world job skills students need to succeed in the workforce. They learn the new exciting Outlook 2016 features by working step by step through practical job-related projects that put the core functionality of Outlook 2016 in context. And as has always been true of the GO! Series, students learn the important concepts when they need them, and they never get lost in the instruction, because the GO! Series uses Microsoft procedural syntax. Students learn how and learn why—at the teachable moment.

Highlights

Easy-to-Follow Chapter Opener includes a detailed introduction to the A & B instructional projects with clearly defined Chapter Objectives and Learning Outcomes.

In-Text Boxed Content: Another Way, Notes, More Knowledge, Alerts, and By Touch instructions, if applicable, are included in line with the instruction and not in the margins, so that students are more likely to read this information.

Visual Chapter Summary focuses on the four key concepts to remember from each chapter.

Review and Assessment Guide summarizes the end-of-chapter assessments for a quick overview of the different types and levels of assignments and assessments for each chapter.

Convenient End-of-Chapter Key Term Glossary with Definitions for each chapter makes reviewing easier.

Instructor Materials

All Instructor and Student materials available at pearsonhighered .com/go

Student Assignment Tracker (previously called Assignment Sheets) – Lists all the assignments for the chapter. Just add the course information, due dates, and points. Providing these to students ensures they will know what is due and when.

Scripted Lectures – A script to guide your classroom lecture of each instructional project.

PowerPoint Lectures – PowerPoint presentations for each chapter.

Prepared Exams – Exams for each chapter.

Test Bank – Includes a variety of test questions for each chapter.

Student Data Files – www.pearsonhighered.com/go.

Syllabus Template – Outlines various plans for covering the content in different length courses.

Getting Started with Microsoft Outlook 2016

PROJECT 1A

OUTCOMES
Receive, respond to, and manage email messages by using Outlook.

OBJECTIVES
1. Start and Navigate Outlook
2. Send and Receive Email
3. Manage Email

PROJECT 1B

OUTCOMES
Manage contact information, task lists, and appointments in Outlook.

OBJECTIVES
4. Create and Edit Contact Records
5. Manage Tasks
6. Manage a Calendar
7. Create a Free Email Account and Use Windows Mail

patcharaporn1984/Fotolia

In This Chapter

Success on the job depends on communicating with others and managing your time. Outlook is the tool to help you do those two things. One of the most common uses of the personal computer is to send and receive email. Email is a convenient way to communicate with coworkers, business contacts, friends, and family members. Outlook combines all the features of a personal information management program with email capabilities. You can use Outlook's email features to send, receive, and forward email messages, and to email files directly from other Microsoft Office programs. You can personalize the messages that you send, and prioritize messages that you send and receive.

The Projects in this chapter relate to **Lake Michigan City College** and the **City of Desert Park, Arizona**. You will use the communications within these two organizations to become familiar with Outlook and practice using Outlook's email capabilities. When you use email for business or personal use, you must manage your email by deleting messages you no longer need, sort and filter messages, and perform other tasks that will keep your Inbox organized. In this chapter, you will practice sending and replying to email messages, managing messages, and printing messages. You will also use Outlook's People, Calendar, and Tasks modules.

PROJECT 1A Manage Email

PROJECT ACTIVITIES

In Activities 1.01 through 1.18, you will set up a mail profile, start Microsoft Outlook 2016, and become familiar with the Outlook modules. Then you will compose, send, read, and respond to email messages for Darron Jacobsen, Vice President of Administrative Affairs at Lake Michigan City College. You will use various Outlook options and manage his email Inbox. You will also print a forwarded message. The messages you send, reply to, and forward will be stored in your Drafts folder rather than being sent to actual recipients. As you progress through the Project, you will insert screenshots of your Inbox, Drafts folder, and one of the printed messages into a PowerPoint presentation similar to Figure 1.1.

PROJECT FILES

For Project 1A, you will need the following files:

o01A_College_Inbox

o01A_Proposed_Schedule

You will save your results in a PowerPoint file as:

Lastname_Firstname_1A_Outlook

PROJECT RESULTS

Outlook 2016, Windows 10, Microsoft Corporation.

Office 2016, Windows 10, Microsoft Corporation.

Office 2016, Windows 10, Microsoft Corporation.

Office 2016, Windows 10, Microsoft Corporation.

Office 2016, Windows 10, Microsoft Corporation.

FIGURE 1.1 Project 1A Manage Email

- Tap an item to click it.
- Press and hold for a few seconds to right-click; release when the information or command displays.
- Touch the screen with two or more fingers and then stretch your fingers apart to zoom in or pinch your fingers together to zoom out.
- Slide your finger on the screen to scroll—slide left to scroll right, slide right to scroll left, slide up to scroll down, slide down to scroll up.
- Slide to rearrange—similar to dragging with a mouse.
- Swipe to select—slide an item a short distance with a quick movement—to select an item and bring up commands, if any.
- On Windows devices, slide a window to the edge or corner of the screen to snap it to that location.
- On Windows devices, swipe from the right edge to display the Action Center or from the left edge to show the Task View of open apps.

Objective 1 | Start and Navigate Outlook

Microsoft Outlook 2016 has two functions: It is an email program, and it is a *personal information manager*. Among other things, a personal information manager enables you to store information about your contacts in electronic form. *Contacts* are friends, family members, coworkers, customers, suppliers, or other individuals with whom you communicate. By using a personal information manager, you can also keep track of your daily schedule, tasks you need to complete, and other information. Outlook's primary modules include Mail for email management and Calendar, People, and Tasks for personal information management.

Outlook stores your email and personal information in folders. There are separate folders for each of Outlook's modules. For example, new email messages that you receive are stored in a folder named *Inbox*; appointments, meetings, and events are stored in a folder named *Calendar*; contact records are stored in a folder named *Contacts*; and tasks are stored in a folder named *Tasks*.

Outlook presents information in *views*, which are ways to look at similar information in different formats and arrangements. Mail, Calendar, People, and Tasks all have different views.

Activity 1.01 | Creating a Mail Profile in Windows

Do you have or use more than one computer? Perhaps you have a computer at home and also a laptop computer that you use at school or when traveling. Maybe you have, or are thinking about getting, a tablet computer. A frustration of working on multiple computers is that they may not look the same. Settings and favorite websites that you have on one PC may not automatically appear on other PCs that you use. Additionally, if you get a new PC, you must try to set it up all over again to look like your old PC.

You can use a *Microsoft account,* which is a single login account for Microsoft systems and services that you can use to sign in to any Windows 10 system. Signing in with a Microsoft account is recommended because you can:

- Download apps from the Windows Store
- Display personalized online content in Windows app tiles
- Sync settings online to make every Windows 10 computer you use look and perform the same

A *user account* is a collection of information that tells Windows what files and folders the account holder can access, what changes the account holder can make to the computer system, and what the account holder's personal preferences are. Each person accesses his or her user account with a user name and password. Each user account has a desktop and a set of private storage folders.

To use a Windows 10 computer, you must establish and then sign in with a user account. The user account can be either a local account or a Microsoft account.

Outlook gets information from the *mail profile* stored in your user account about the email accounts it should connect to when it starts. A mail profile stores information about your email accounts and the associated data file locations. For purposes of this instruction, it is recommended that you create a new mail profile so that your own email, contacts, calendar items, and tasks are not intermingled with those of the Projects you will complete in this textbook.

ALERT!   **Creating a Mail Profile**

Create a new mail profile as described in the following steps to complete this instruction. Doing so will ensure that information from your own email account is not modified by this instruction. You can complete this Activity if you signed in to Windows by using a local account or a Microsoft account. It is not necessary to have administrative rights on the computer to complete the steps in this Activity.

---

1 Be sure that the Outlook program is closed; if necessary, **Close** ☒ the Outlook window.

2 On the Windows taskbar, click in the search box, type **control panel** and then in the list of search results, click **Control Panel Desktop app** to display the **Control Panel** window.

3 In the upper right corner of the window, click the **View by arrow**, and then click **Small icons**. Notice that the items on the screen are in alphabetic order from left to right.

4 Locate and click **Mail (Microsoft Outlook 2016)** to display the **Mail Setup – Outlook** dialog box. Compare your screen with Figure 1.2. (If you see the dialog box in Figure 1.3, move to Step 6.)

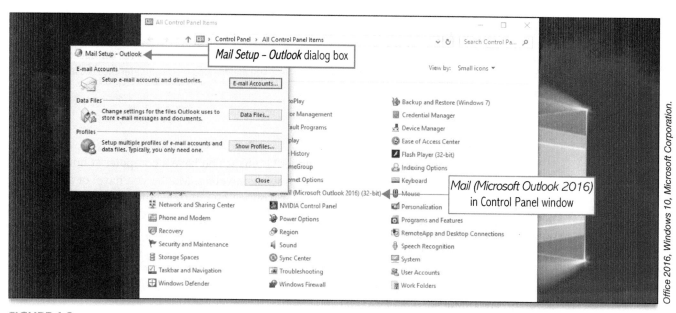

FIGURE 1.2

Office 2016, Windows 10, Microsoft Corporation.

5 Under **Profiles**, click **Show Profiles** to display the **Mail** dialog box listing all the Outlook profiles currently configured for your user account.

6 Under **When starting Microsoft Outlook, use this profile**, click the **Prompt for a profile to be used** option button, and then in the middle portion of the dialog box, click **Add** to display the **New Profile** dialog box. Compare your screen with Figure 1.3.

Outlook 2016, Windows 10, Microsoft Corporation.

FIGURE 1.3

7 In the **Profile Name** box, type **GO-** followed by your first name and last name, and then click **OK** to create the new profile and start the **Add Account** wizard.

You will save the new profile and exit Control Panel before starting Activity 1.02.

8 In the **Add Account** wizard, click **Cancel**, and then in the **Microsoft Outlook** message box shown in Figure 1.4, click **OK**.

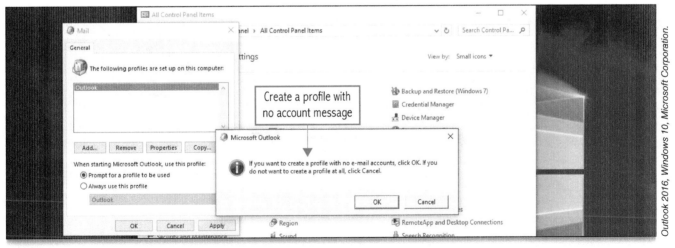

Outlook 2016, Windows 10, Microsoft Corporation.

FIGURE 1.4

In the **Mail** dialog box, notice that the profile name you just created displays, as shown in Figure 1.5. Click **OK**. Then **Close** ☒ the **Control Panel** window.

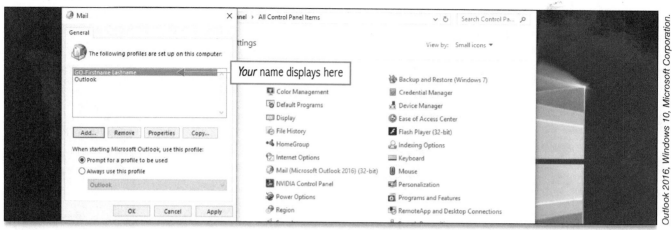

FIGURE 1.5

Activity 1.02 | Configuring Outlook to Connect to an Email Account

The Mail profile configured for your Windows user account stores information about you and the email accounts that you connect to from Outlook. Additionally, Outlook creates an Outlook Data File for each email account that you connect to. You can connect to more than one email account per profile so that you can manage email communications for multiple accounts within Outlook.

 On the Windows taskbar, click in the search box, type **outlook** and then in the list of search results, click **Outlook 2016 Desktop app** to start Outlook on your desktop. In the **Choose Profile** dialog box, click the **Profile Name arrow**, and then click the profile name that you just created. Compare your screen with Figure 1.6.

In Activity 1.01, you configured Outlook to prompt you to select a profile when starting.

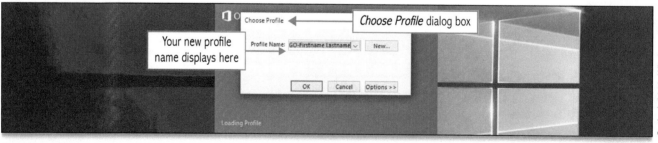

FIGURE 1.6

2 In the **Choose Profile** dialog box, click **OK**, and then compare your screen with Figure 1.7.

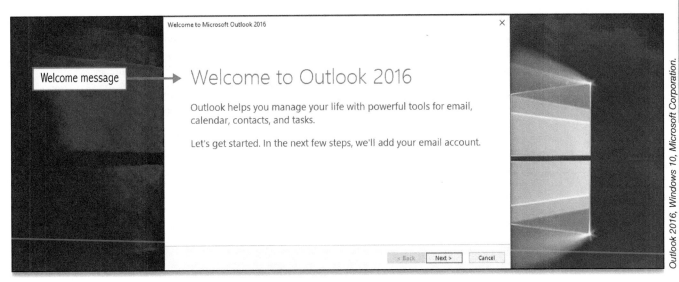

FIGURE 1.7

3 Below the **Welcome to Outlook 2016** message, click **Next**.

Here you can configure Outlook to connect to an email account by providing the account *credentials*—the email address and account password. Because you will use fictitious information in this instruction, it is not necessary to connect to a real email account.

4 Under **Do you want to set up Outlook to connect to an email account**, click **No**, and then click **Next**.

5 In the **Cancel Email Account Setup** dialog box, select the **Use Outlook without an email account** check box, and then compare your screen with Figure 1.8.

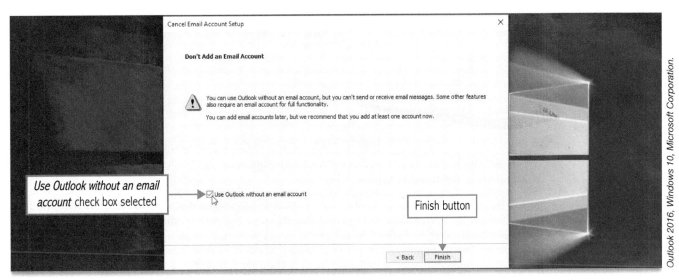

FIGURE 1.8

6 Click **Finish**.

7 If Outlook prompts you to do so, type the Administrator password, and then click Yes. In the upper right corner, if the Outlook window does not fill the screen, **Maximize** ☐ the window, and then compare your screen with Figure 1.9.

Outlook Today is a single screen that summarizes the day's calendar events and scheduled tasks associated with the default email account. You can display the Outlook Today view for an email account at any time by clicking the account data file header in the Folder Pane.

Because the user interface colors and ribbon background depend on settings that were established when Office was configured on the computer you are using, your colors and ribbon background may differ from what is shown in the Figure.

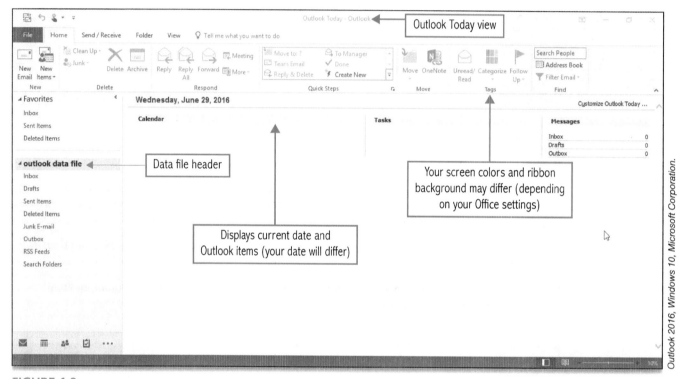

FIGURE 1.9

Activity 1.03 | Exploring Outlook

1 On the left side of the Outlook window, under **outlook data file**, click **Inbox**. Compare your screen with Figure 1.10, and then take a moment to study the descriptions of the screen elements in the table in Figure 1.11.

This is the *Mail module*, where Outlook manages your messages. By default, the Mail module displays the Folder Pane, Navigation Bar, message list, and Reading Pane. The message list, located to the right of the Folder Pane, displays your email messages. On the right side of the screen, the Reading Pane displays a preview of the currently selected message. If your Inbox contains no messages, the Reading Pane is blank. You can also choose not to display wthe Reading Pane.

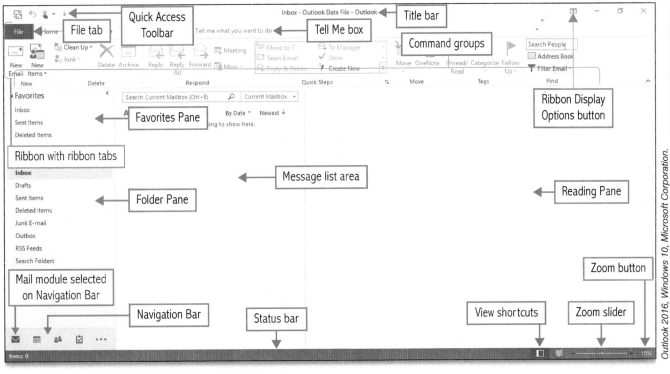

FIGURE 1.10

MICROSOFT OUTLOOK SCREEN ELEMENTS	
SCREEN ELEMENT	**DESCRIPTION**
Favorites Pane	Provides quick access to your primary Inbox and Sent Items folders and any other folders you want to add to it.
File tab	Displays Backstage view, a centralized space for managing Outlook and email account settings.
Folder Pane	Displays in every Outlook module—Mail, Calendar, People, and Tasks—to display folders related to the module.
Message list area	In the Inbox, displays your received messages in the currently active view.
Navigation Bar	Displays navigation controls at the bottom of the Folder Pane.
Quick Access Toolbar	Displays buttons to perform frequently used commands with a single click. In the program window, the default buttons include Send/Receive All Folders and Undo. In Outlook item windows, the default buttons include Save, Undo, Redo/Repeat, Previous Item, and Next Item. You can add and delete buttons to customize the Quick Access Toolbar for your convenience.
Reading Pane	Displays the content of the currently selected item. Also displays draft message responses unless you open them in separate message windows.
Ribbon	Displays task-oriented tabs that contain groups of commands, styles, and resources you need to work in Outlook. The look of your ribbon depends on your screen resolution. At a higher resolution, the ribbon will be wider and will display more individual items and button names.
Ribbon Display Options	A button for controlling the display of the ribbon tabs and commands.
Ribbon groups	On the ribbon, a named set of commands that are related to a specific type of object, item, or action.
Ribbon tabs	On the ribbon, a page of commands that are related to a specific type of task.
Status bar	Displays and provides access to information about items in the current view, reminders, group notifications, view shortcuts, and zoom controls.
Tell Me box	Finds Outlook commands that match the search term you enter, and links to related Outlook Help articles and online search results.
Title bar	Displays the Quick Access Toolbar (in its default location), the program name, and the program window control buttons—Minimize, Maximize/Restore Down, and Close.
Zoom button	Displays the current magnification and opens the Zoom dialog box.
Zoom slider	Controls the magnification of the Reading Pane content.

FIGURE 1.11

2 If the Favorites Pane is open in the upper portion of the **Folder Pane**, click ◢ to the left of **Favorites** to collapse the pane.

The button changes ▷ to indicate that the pane is closed.

3 Below the **Folder Pane**, on the **Navigation Bar**, click **Calendar** ▦, and then compare your screen with Figure 1.12.

This is the ***Calendar module***, where Outlook displays and manages your appointments, meetings, and events. By default, the Calendar module displays a view of the current month.

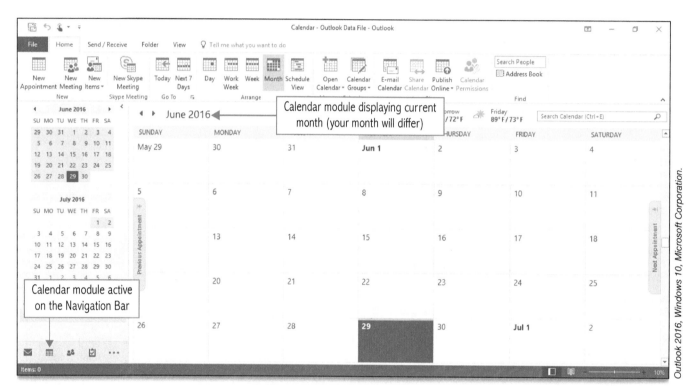

FIGURE 1.12

4 On the **Navigation Bar**, click **People** ▪▪, and then compare your screen with Figure 1.13.

This is the ***People module***, where Outlook displays and manages information about your contacts—individuals about whom you have information such as email addresses, mailing addresses, phone numbers, fax numbers, and webpages. When you create a contact or import contact records from other systems, the contact records display in the middle pane of the Outlook window.

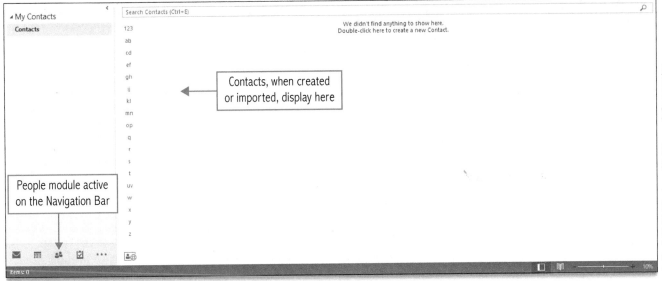

FIGURE 1.13

> 5 ▸ On the **Navigation Bar**, click **Tasks** ☑, and then compare your screen with Figure 1.14.

> This is the *Tasks module*, where Outlook displays and manages tasks and Outlook items you flag to do something with. By default, the Tasks module displays your To-Do List, which includes both tasks and flagged items. Until you create a task, accept a task assignment, or flag an item for follow-up, the list is blank.

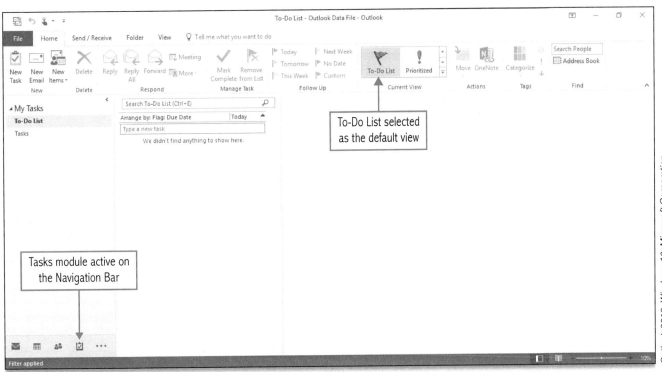

FIGURE 1.14

> 6 ▸ On the **Navigation Bar**, click **Mail** ✉ to return to the Inbox.

To send an email message to someone, you must know the recipient's email address. There are two parts to an email address—the first part is the user account name. The second part is the **domain name**, which is the host name of the recipient's mail server; for example, Microsoft's outlook.com or Google's gmail.com. A domain name can also be specific to an organization such as a school or business. The user account name and domain name are separated by the symbol @, which is called the **at sign**.

Activity 1.04 | Configuring Outlook for Sending and Receiving Messages

When your computer is **online**—connected to your organization's network or to the Internet—Outlook's default setting is to send messages immediately when you click the Send button in a Message form, and to store copies of the sent messages in the Sent Items folder. When your computer is **offline**—not connected to a network or to the Internet—Outlook stores messages in the Outbox until the computer is online and Outlook can send the message.

1. Click the **File tab** to display **Backstage** view, and then in the left pane, click **Options** to display the **Outlook Options** dialog box. In the page list on the left side of the dialog box, click the **Advanced** page tab.

2. In the vertical scroll bar on the right side of the **Outlook Options** dialog box, click the **down scroll arrow** or drag the scroll box down until the section with the heading *Send and receive* is visible. Clear the **Send immediately when connected** check box, and then compare your screen with Figure 1.15.

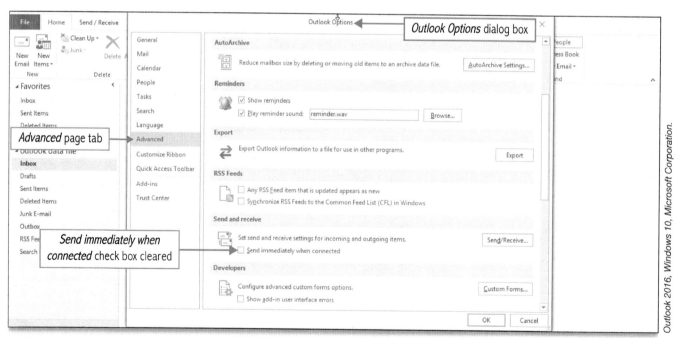

FIGURE 1.15

3 On the right side of the **Send and receive** section of the dialog box, click **Send/Receive**.

4 In the **Send/Receive Groups** dialog box, under **Setting for group "All Accounts"**, clear the **Include this group in send/receive (F9)** and **Schedule an automatic send/receive every** check boxes.

5 Under **When Outlook is Offline**, clear the **Include this group in send/receive (F9)** check box, and then compare your screen with Figure 1.16.

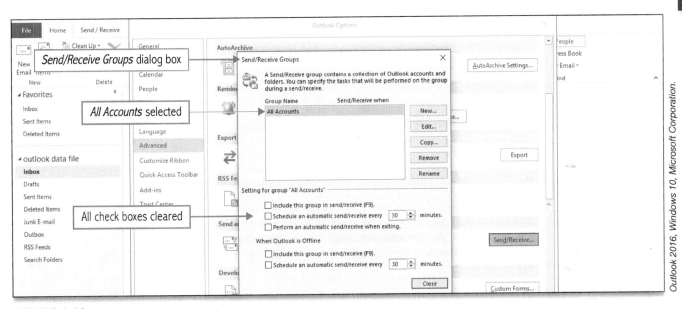

FIGURE 1.16

6 Click **Close**, and then in the **Outlook Options** dialog box, click **OK** to close the dialog box.

Activity 1.05 | Creating and Sending a New Email Message

When creating email messages, Outlook uses the Microsoft Word editor to manage the formatting of the message content. This means that you can use many Word features when creating message content; for example, you can easily create lists and tables, insert graphics, and check the spelling of the message text. In this Activity, you will create a message from Darron Jacobsen to one of his colleagues at Lake Michigan City College.

1 In the **Folder Pane**, click **Inbox**. On the **Home tab**, in the **New group**, click **New Email**, and then compare your screen with Figure 1.17.

The Message has a ribbon that contains commands specific to the creation of messages and message content. The commands are organized in groups on different tabs of the ribbon.

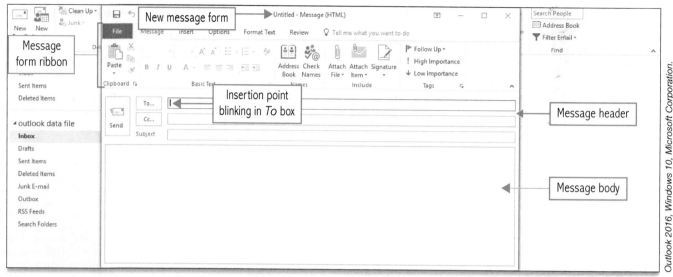

FIGURE 1.17

2 In the **To** box, type **LHuelsman@LakeMichCityCollege.edu**

This is the email address of the recipient. *Syntax* refers to the way in which the parts of the email address are put together. The user account name is to the left of the @ symbol, and the domain name is on the right. If another student has used the computer at which you are working, the Outlook AutoComplete feature might display Ms. Huelsman's complete email address after you begin typing it.

3 In the **Cc** box, click to place the insertion point, and then type **HSabaj@LakeMichCityCollege.edu**

Outlook sends a *courtesy copy* of the message to the address specified in the Cc box. Send a courtesy copy to people who need to see the message but probably do not need to reply. You can enter multiple addresses in the To and the Cc boxes, separating each address with a semicolon.

4 Click to place the insertion point in the **Subject** box, and then type **Chamber of Commerce presentation**

You can move the insertion point from one box to another either by clicking in the box or by pressing Tab.

> **NOTE** **Underlined Email Addresses**
>
> By default, after you type an email address in the To or Cc box, Outlook verifies that the address has the correct syntax and then underlines the address. If the email address is associated with a contact that you saved in the People module, Outlook changes the email address to the "Display As" entry for the contact, which may be a name, an email address, a combination of the two, or another identifier that you specify.

---

5 Click to place the insertion point in the message body of the Message form. Type **Hi Lisa,** and then press Enter two times.

This is the beginning of your message. It is considered good etiquette to include an appropriate salutation and to address the recipient(s) by name. Keep your messages short and to the point. It is usually helpful to the recipient if you restrict your message to only one topic. If you have another topic to discuss, send another email message that has a Subject entry specific to that topic.

6 Type **I just received confirmation from the Chamber of Commerce; they would like to have you speak at their next monthly meeting. Let's arrange a time for us to meet and discuss your presentation. I'd like Henry to meet with us as well.**

7 Press ⟨Enter⟩ two times and type **You might want to look at Joyce's presentation from last month when she spoke at the Illinois Special Needs Teachers Conference. If you don't have a copy of it, Mary can lend you hers.**

> When you want to leave a single blank line between paragraphs, press ⟨Enter⟩ two times.

> When typing your message, do not indent the first line of paragraphs, and press ⟨Spacebar⟩ only one time following the punctuation at the end of a sentence.

8 Press ⟨Enter⟩ **two** times, type **Darron** and then click somewhere in the text of the message away from the name.

> *Darron* is flagged with a wavy red line, indicating that the word is not in the standard Microsoft Office dictionary. Proper names are often not in the dictionary; however, this is the correct spelling of Mr. Jacobsen's name.

9 Right-click *Darron* to display a shortcut menu of actions related to the word. On the shortcut menu, below the list of suggested spelling corrections, click **Ignore All**.

10 Press ⟨Ctrl⟩ + ⟨Home⟩ to move the insertion point to the beginning of the message, and then compare your message window with Figure 1.18.

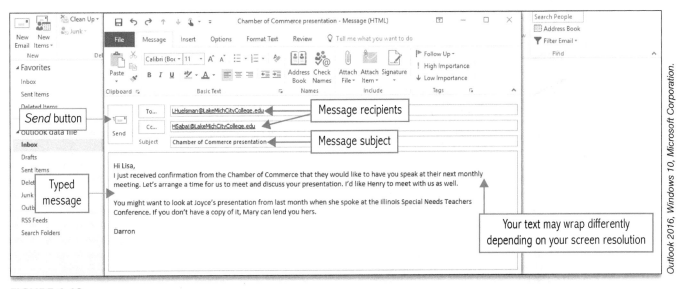

FIGURE 1.18

11 At the left end of the message header, click **Send**. In the **Microsoft Outlook** message box that displays, click **Add Account**, and then at the bottom of the **Add Account** dialog box, click **Cancel**. (Or, if the Connect Outlook to Office 365 window displays, close it.)

> Because you have not configured Outlook to connect to an email account, Outlook saves your message in the Drafts folder. A *draft* is a temporary copy of a message that has not yet been sent.

12 Take a moment to study the table in Figure 1.19 that describes how you can use keyboard shortcuts to move the insertion point in the body of your email message.

KEYBOARD SHORTCUTS FOR MOVING THE INSERTION POINT IN A MESSAGE	
KEYBOARD SHORTCUT	**RESULT**
Ctrl + Home	Moves the insertion point to the beginning of the message
Ctrl + End	Moves the insertion point to the end of the message
Home	Moves the insertion point to the beginning of the line
End	Moves the insertion point to the end of the line
↑	Moves the insertion point up one line
↓	Moves the insertion point down one line
PageUp	Moves the insertion point up one window
PageDown	Moves the insertion point down one window

Outlook 2016, Windows 10, Microsoft Corporation.

FIGURE 1.19

Activity 1.06 │ Importing Messages to the Inbox

In this Activity, you will *import* Darron Jacobsen's received messages into your Inbox. To import means to bring the information into Outlook from another program in which the information already exists. You can import messages, contacts, and calendar events by using the method described in this instruction.

1 In the **Folder Pane**, click **Inbox**.

2 Click the **File tab**, and then in the left pane, click **Open & Export**. Under **Open**, click **Import/Export**, and then compare your screen with Figure 1.20.

The Import and Export Wizard dialog box displays. A *wizard* is a tool that walks you through a process step by step.

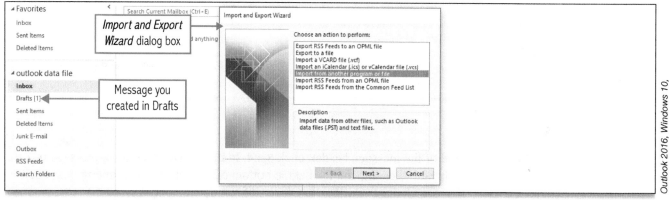

Outlook 2016, Windows 10, Microsoft Corporation.

FIGURE 1.20

3 In the **Import and Export Wizard** dialog box, under **Choose an action to perform**, click **Import from another program or file**, and then click **Next**.

4 In the **Import a File** dialog box, under **Select file type to import from**, click **Outlook Data File (.pst)**, and then click **Next**.

5 In the **Import Outlook Data File** dialog box, click **Browse**.

6 In the displayed **Open Outlook Data Files** dialog box, navigate to the location where you have stored the student data files that accompany this textbook. Locate **o01A_College_Inbox**, and click one time to select it. Then, in the lower right corner of the **Open Outlook Data Files** dialog box, click **Open**.

The Open Outlook Data Files dialog box closes, and the path and file name display in the File to import box.

7 In the **Import Outlook Data File** dialog box, click **Next**.

8 Under **Select the folder to import from**, click the **Personal Folders** arrow to expand the data file, and then click the **Inbox** folder.

The Import Outlook Data File dialog box displays the folder structure for the file you are going to import.

9 Below the **Select the folder to import from** pane, click the **Import items into the current folder** option button. Compare your screen with Figure 1.21.

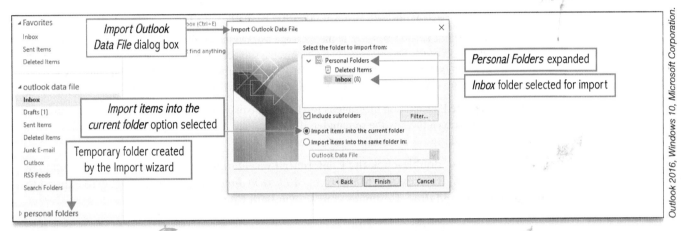

Outlook 2016, Windows 10, Microsoft Corporation.

FIGURE 1.21

10 Click **Finish**. If necessary, on the **View tab**, in the **Layout group**, click **Reading Pane**, and then click **Right** to display the pane. Compare your screen with Figure 1.22.

This fictitious information does not use current dates.

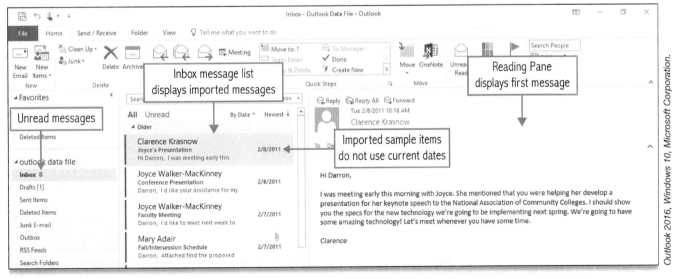

Outlook 2016, Windows 10, Microsoft Corporation.

FIGURE 1.22

You can read messages in two ways. You can read a message in the Reading Pane without opening the message, or you can open the message in a separate message window. In this Activity, you will view Darron Jacobsen's messages in several ways.

1 Look at the **Inbox**, and take a moment to study the messages shown.

In the Folder Pane, the number to the right of *Inbox* represents the number of unread messages in that folder. In the Mail module, the message list to the right of the Folder Pane displays messages and received items, and the Reading Pane to the right of the message list displays the content of the selected message or item.

The ***message header*** is visible in the message list and in the Reading Pane. The header for each message includes information about the message such as the sender, subject, and date received. Additional message header details are included in the message's properties.

2 In the **Inbox**, locate the second message, which is from Joyce Walker-MacKinney and has the subject *Conference Presentation*. Click it one time to display it in the **Reading Pane** on the right.

When you select the second message in the message list, Outlook removes the bold formatting from the sender and subject of the first message and changes the subject color from blue to black. These changes indicate that Outlook considers the message status as read (rather than unread). When you view a message in the Reading Pane, Outlook sets its status to read when you move to another message.

The Conference Presentation message is too long to display entirely in the Reading Pane; however, you can scroll down to view the remainder of the message. Or, you may prefer to open the message to read it.

3 In the **message list**, double-click the **Conference Presentation** message to open it in a separate message window. If necessary, to the right of *Darron Jacobsen,* click the arrow to expand to display the date and time. Compare your screen with Figure 1.23.

ANOTHER WAY Use the keyboard shortcut **Ctrl** + **O** to open a message in a message window.

The open message window has a ribbon that displays commands related specifically to processing the received message. Above the ribbon, the title bar displays the message subject, and the Quick Access Toolbar displays buttons for saving the message and moving to the previous or next message. The message header includes the date and time the message was sent and the message sender, subject, and recipients.

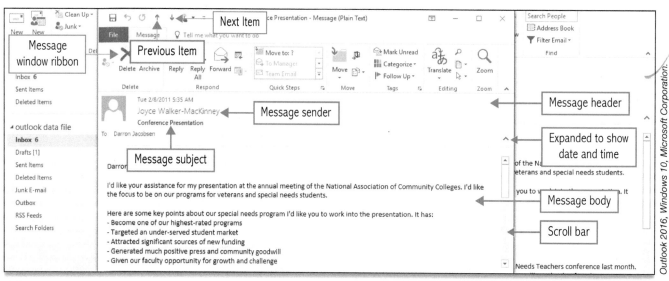

FIGURE 1.23

4 In the vertical scroll bar to the right of the message body, click the **down scroll arrow** ▼ or drag the scroll box down until the end of the message displays.

5 In the upper right corner of the message window, click **Close** ✕.

6 In the **Inbox**, locate the third message, which is from Joyce Walker-MacKinney and has the subject *Faculty Meeting*. Double-click the message to open it.

7 In the message window, on the **Quick Access Toolbar**, click the **Previous Item** ↑ button.

In the displayed message window, the *Faculty Meeting* message is replaced by the previous message in your Inbox, the *Conference Presentation* message.

8 On the **Quick Access Toolbar**, click the **Next Item** ↓ button two times.

In the displayed message window, the *Conference Presentation* message is replaced first by the *Faculty Meeting* message, and then by the next message in your Inbox, which has the subject *Fall/Intersession Schedule*. You can view all the messages in your Inbox in the message window by using these Quick Access Toolbar buttons. Each message replaces the previous one in the displayed message window.

9 Click the **Next Item** ↓ button seven times to view the remaining messages in the Inbox. The last message is from Henry Sabaj and has the subject heading *Alumnus Honored*.

10 **Close** ✕ the message window, and notice that no unread items remain in the Inbox.

Activity 1.08 | Viewing and Opening a Message Attachment

A message might include an ***attachment***, which is a separate file that is included with the message. One of the messages Darron has received includes an attachment.

1 In the **Inbox**, locate the message from Mary Adair with the subject *Fall/Intersession Schedule* and click it one time to display it in the **Reading Pane**. Compare your screen with Figure 1.24.

In the message list, a small paper clip icon displays above the date of the message. This indicates that the message has an attachment. In the Reading Pane, between the message header and message body, a rectangle represents the message attachment. The attachment is labeled with the Word program icon to indicate that it is a Word document, the file name, and the file size.

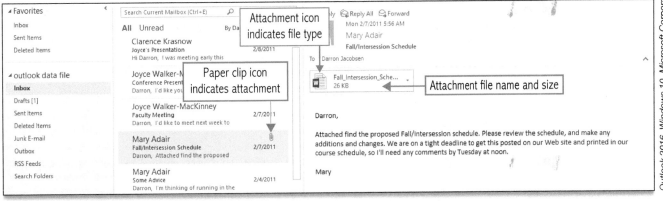

FIGURE 1.24

2 In the **Reading Pane**, point to the attachment to display the full file name, file type, and file size in a ScreenTip.

3 In the **Reading Pane**, click the attachment one time to preview it in the message body. Compare your screen with Figure 1.25.

You can preview and scroll through Office files, text files, HTML files, RTF files, PDF files, XPS files, and some other attachment file types directly in the Reading Pane. A full list of the available attachment previewers is available from the Attachment Handling page of the Outlook Options Trust Center.

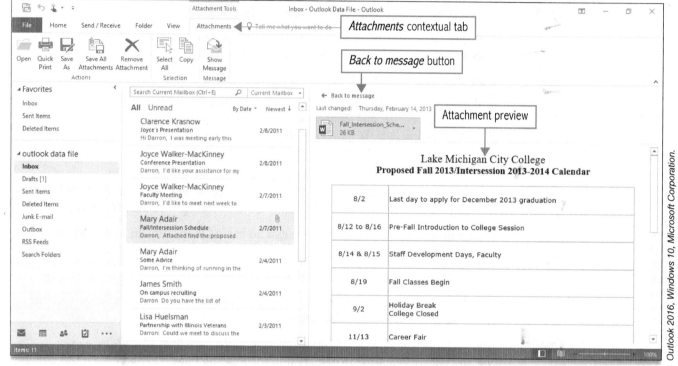

FIGURE 1.25

4 At the top of the **Reading Pane**, click **Back to message** to redisplay the message text.

An attachment is part of an email message unless you save it separately. You can save an attachment separately by clicking the arrow ▾ on the right side of the attachment icon in the Reading Pane and then clicking Save As. You will not save this attachment separately.

5 In the **Reading Pane**, below the message header, double-click the file attachment to open it in Microsoft Word. If any Word or Office introductory screens open in front of the document, close them.

The Word program starts and displays the attached file, which is a Word document.

Because you are opening the document from an email message, a banner might display across the top of the document informing you that Word has opened the document in Protected View. Protected View is a security feature of Word. You can manage Protected View settings from the Word Options Trust Center.

6 In the upper right corner of the **Microsoft Word** title bar, click **Close** ☒ to close the attachment.

More Knowledge   **Blocked File Attachments**

Outlook automatically blocks the receipt of over 80 types of file attachments that might contain malware. For example, any file that has the file name extension of .asp, .bat, .cmd, .exe, .hta, .js, .msi, or .vbs is blocked. If you use Outlook to connect to a Microsoft Exchange Server email account and you need to receive blocked files of a specific file type through email, the Exchange Server administrator might be able to unblock the file type for you. It is often easier and safer to transfer files by using another method such as downloading files from an FTP site, a Dropbox folder, or a SharePoint library instead of risking the possibility of allowing malware into the Exchange Server system.

You can reply to an email message from the Inbox or while viewing it in a message window. When replying from the Inbox, the Reply button is available on the Home tab in the Respond group, and in the Reading Pane. In a message window, the Reply button is located on the Message tab in the Respond group. In this Activity, you will send a reply to one of the messages that Darron Jacobsen received.

1 In the **Inbox**, select the message from James Smith that has the subject *On campus recruiting* to display it in the **Reading Pane**. Then, on the **Home tab**, in the **Respond group**, click **Reply**. Compare your screen with Figure 1.26.

Outlook creates the reply message in the Reading Pane and displays a Message contextual tab that contains the most common message composition–related commands. You can "pop out" the reply message into a message window if you want to access the full message window ribbon. In the reply message, Outlook places the sender's email address in the To box and adds the prefix **RE:** to the message subject, which is commonly used in correspondence to mean *in regard to* or *regarding*. The text of the original message is included in the message body, with space above it to enter your response.

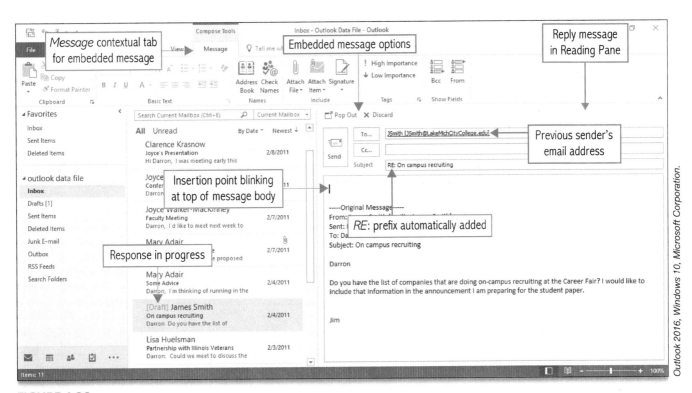

FIGURE 1.26

2 With the insertion point at the top of the message body, type **Jim,** and press Enter two times. Type **I will have the list ready for you by the end of the day.** Press Enter two times, and type **Darron**

Your reply appears above the original message so that the recipient does not have to scroll down to see it.

3 In the upper left corner of the reply message, click **Send**. Click **Add Account**, and then click **Cancel** (or click **Close** ☒ in the Connect message) to place the reply message in the **Drafts** folder.

Recall that because Outlook is not connected to an email account, you are placing all outgoing messages in the Drafts folder.

Activity 1.10 | Forwarding an Email Message

You can *forward* an email message you receive to someone else. However, do not forward messages to others unless you are sure the sender of the original message would approve of forwarding the message. You can forward a message from the Inbox or while viewing it in a message window. Darron Jacobsen has received a message that he wants to forward to another person, Henry Sabaj at Lake Michigan City College.

1 In the **Inbox message list**, scroll up as necessary, and then click the message from Joyce Walker-MacKinney that has the subject *Faculty Meeting*.

2 In the **Reading Pane**, above the message header, click the **Forward** button.

Outlook creates the forward message in the Reading Pane and adds the prefix *FW:* to the message subject. The text of the original message is included in the message body, with space above it to append your comments.

3 In the **To** box, type **h**—the first letter of the recipient's address—and then compare your screen with Figure 1.27.

In a list under the To box, Outlook displays the address *HSabaj@LakeMichCityCollege.edu*, which you entered in the Cc box in Activity 1.05. This is an example of Outlook's *AutoComplete* feature; Outlook remembers email addresses you have typed previously, and displays a list of addresses that match the characters as you type them in the To or Cc box. You can choose an address from the list, or continue typing if the address you want isn't in the list.

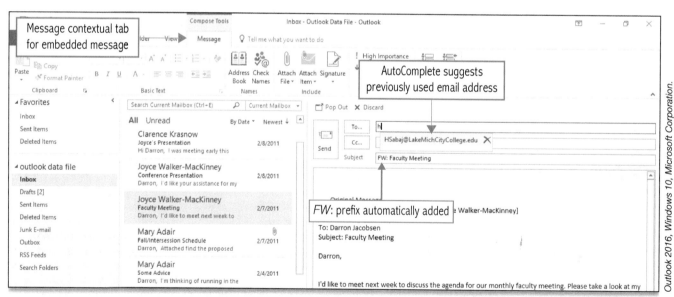

FIGURE 1.27

4 Point to the *HSabaj* email address and click one time, or, if the address is highlighted in the AutoComplete list, press Enter to place it in the **To** box.

5 Click to place the insertion point at the top of the message body, type **Henry,** and then press Enter two times.

6 Type **As you can see from Joyce's message below, she's asked me to find out if you have any outstanding issues for the next faculty meeting.** Press [Enter] two times, and type **Let me know.**

7 Press [Enter] two times and type **Darron** Then click **Send**, click **Add Account**, and click **Cancel** (or click **Close** ☒ in the Connect message) to place the forwarded message in the **Drafts** folder.

Activity 1.11 | Sending a Message with an Attachment

You can attach one or more files to any message you send, including replies and forwarded messages. When you reply to a message, you may prefer not to include some, or all, of the previous message. You can delete portions of text by *selecting text* (by dragging across it with the mouse pointer) and pressing [Delete].

1 In the **message list**, double-click the Henry Sabaj *RE: Schedule* message to display it in a message window. On the **Message tab**, in the **Respond group**, click **Reply** to create a reply message in a new message window.

The original message subject indicates Henry sent it as a reply to another message.

2 In the message body, scroll down as necessary, and click to place the insertion point at the beginning of the line that contains the second instance of *Original Message*. Drag downward to select the original message, and then compare your screen with Figure 1.28.

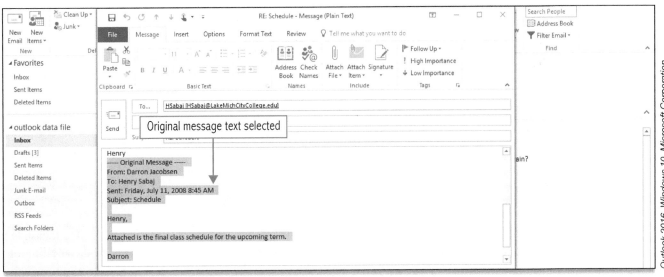

FIGURE 1.28

3 Press [Delete] to delete the selected text.

4 Press [Ctrl] + [Home] to move the insertion point to the beginning of the message body. Type **Henry,** and then press [Enter] two times.

5 Type **Here it is again.** Press [Enter] two times and then type **Darron** On the **Message tab**, in the **Include group**, click **Attach File**.

The Attach File menu displays a list of files you worked with recently, and the Browse Web Locations and Browse This PC commands.

6 At the bottom of the **Attach File** menu, click **Browse This PC**. In the displayed **Insert File** dialog box, navigate to the location where the student files that accompany this textbook are stored. Locate and click the Word file **o01A_Proposed_Schedule**. Then, in the lower right corner of the **Insert File** dialog box, click **Insert**. Compare your reply message window with Figure 1.29.

The Insert File dialog box closes, and the message redisplays with the document attached to it. The Word icon and the name of the attached file display next to the word *Attached* in the lower portion of the message header. If you attach a file to a message and then decide later you that do not want to send the file, you can click the attachment icon and press Delete to detach the file from the message.

FIGURE 1.29

Outlook 2016, Windows 10, Microsoft Corporation.

7 Click **Send**, click **Add Account**, and then click **Cancel** (or click **Close** ☒ in the Connect message) to place the reply message in the **Drafts** folder.

8 **Close** ☒ the original message.

Objective 3 | Manage Email

Outlook has options that you can apply to messages. For example, you can mark a message to remind yourself or the message recipient to take follow-up action. You can check the spelling of message content before you send it. You can indicate the sensitivity or importance of a message. *Sensitivity* refers to message content that should be kept private—for example, information about employee salaries. *Importance* refers to the urgency of the message—for example, you can indicate that a message should be read immediately or can be read later.

Activity 1.12 | Marking Messages and Formatting Text

Marking messages as *unread* is one way to draw attention to a message within your message list. Marking a message with a flag—referred to as *flagging*—gives you another way to draw attention to a message and to include additional information with it. You can flag sent and received messages, and you can flag outgoing messages. *Formatting text* refers to the process of changing the appearance of the text in a message. In this Activity, you will mark a previously read message as unread and reply to one of Darron Jacobsen's received messages, adding a flag and formatting the reply.

1 ▶ If necessary, display the **Inbox**. In the **message list**, locate the message from Mary Adair that has the subject *Purchase Order*—you might have to scroll down ▾ to see this message. Point to the message, right-click, and then on the shortcut menu, click **Mark as Unread**.

Use this command to change a previously read message back to an unread message. A blue bar displays to the left of the message in the message list, and the subject changes to bold, blue text.

2 ▶ In the **message list**, locate the message from Clarence Krasnow with the subject *Joyce's Presentation*, and then double-click it to open it in a message window.

3 ▶ On the **Message tab**, in the **Respond group**, click **Reply**. On the **Format Text tab**, in the **Format group**, click **HTML**.

(HTML) displays on the message window title bar after the message subject. You can apply formatting to the text of messages you compose in HTML or Rich Text format.

4 ▶ With the insertion point at the top of the message body, type **Clarence,** and then press ⏎ two times. Type **This sounds like a great idea. Let's meet at 3:00 tomorrow in my office. I will put it on my schedule.** Press ⏎ two times, and then type **Let me know if this is OK with you.** Press ⏎ two times, and then type **Darron**

5 ▶ Select the sentence *Let me know if this is OK with you.* On the displayed mini toolbar, click **Italic** ☐*I*☐ to apply italic formatting to the selected text. Click the **Font Size button arrow**, and then click **12** to increase the font size. Click anywhere in the message to cancel the text selection. Compare your screen with Figure 1.30.

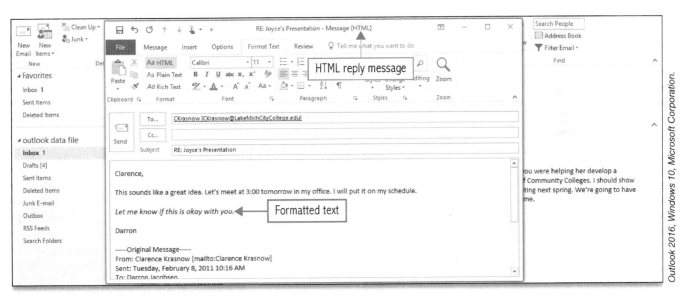

Outlook 2016, Windows 10, Microsoft Corporation.

FIGURE 1.30

6 ▸ On the **Message tab**, in the **Tags group**, click **Follow Up** 🚩, and then click **Add Reminder**. Compare your screen with Figure 1.31.

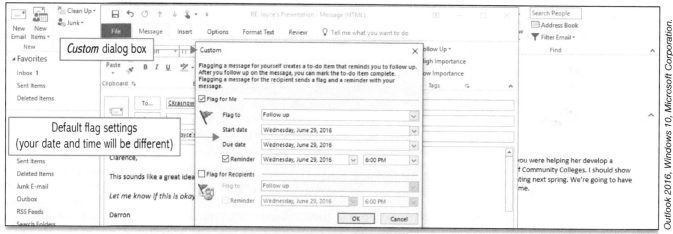

FIGURE 1.31

7 ▸ In the **Custom** dialog box, under **Flag for Me**, click the **Flag to arrow** to view a predefined list of requested actions you can add to the message. Scroll to the bottom of the **Flag to** list, and click **Review**.

By default, the flag is set only for the message sender. You can use any of the default actions. Notice that you can also specify a date and time.

8 ▸ In the **Custom** dialog box, select the **Flag for Recipients check box**.

9 ▸ Under **Flag for Recipients**, from the **Flag to** list, click **Reply**. Then select the **Reminder** check box.

If the message recipient uses Outlook, a reminder to reply to the message will display on the recipient's system at the appropriate time.

10 ▸ In the lower right corner of the **Custom** dialog box, click **OK**. Compare your screen with Figure 1.32.

Information about the flags you set for yourself and the message recipient displays in the message header.

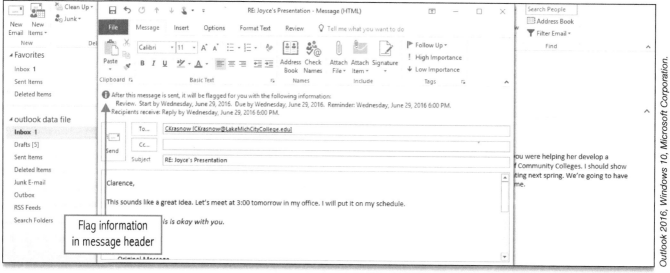

FIGURE 1.32

11 ▸ In the message header, click **Send**. Click **Add Account**, and then click **Cancel** (or click **Close** ☒ in the Connect message) to place the reply message in the Drafts folder. **Close** ☒ the original message.

12 ▸ In the **message list**, select the message from James Smith with the subject *Lunch*. Notice that a red flag displays by the date.

> This is how a flagged message appears to the recipient. In the Reading Pane, at the bottom of the message header, a banner indicates that the flag is to *Follow up*.

13 ▸ In the **message list**, select the message from Joyce Walker-MacKinney with the subject *Conference Presentation*. On the **Home tab**, in the **Tags group**, click **Follow Up**, and then click the **Tomorrow** flag.

> A flag displays in the message list and a banner displays at the bottom of the message header.

Activity 1.13 | Using the Spelling Checker

Outlook uses the automatic spelling and grammar checker that is common to all Office programs. The spelling and grammar checker is active when Outlook is installed. Outlook indicates a misspelled word in a message as you compose it by underlining it with a wavy red line. To view a list of suggested corrections for a word that has a wavy red line, right-click the word. In this Activity, you will send a new message from Darron Jacobsen to one of his colleagues and use the spelling checker to find and correct spelling errors.

1 ▸ On the **Home tab**, in the **New group**, click **New Email**. In the **To** box, type **LHuelsman@LakeMichCityCollege.edu**. As you type, if the email address displays as a ScreenTip, indicating that Outlook remembers it, you can press ⌷Enter⌷ to have the AutoComplete feature fill in the address for you.

2 ▸ Press ⌷Tab⌷ two times to move the insertion point to the **Subject** box. Type **Let's meet with the VA** and then press ⌷Tab⌷ one time to place the insertion point in the message body.

> Recall that it is a good email practice to create a subject that is brief and informative for recipients when they view your message in a list of other received messages.

3 ▸ In the message area, type **Lisa,** and then press ⌷Enter⌷ two times.

4 ▸ Type, but do not correct any spelling errors, as follows: **I'm arranging a meeting with the Illanois Veterans Association to discuss our partnerchip program. Could you join me?** Press ⌷Enter⌷ two times and type **Darron**

> Outlook indicates that the words *Illanois* and *partnerchip* are misspelled by underlining them with wavy red lines. You can have Outlook provide the correct spellings.

5 Right-click the word **Illanois** and then compare your screen with Figure 1.33.

A shortcut menu displays near the pointer. At the top of the shortcut menu, Outlook suggests a correct spelling of the word. If there is more than one possible correct spelling, the shortcut menu displays multiple choices.

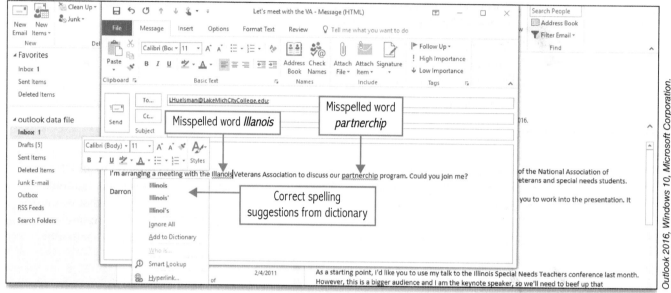

FIGURE 1.33

6 At the top of the shortcut menu, click **Illinois** to replace the misspelled word with the correct spelling.

7 Right-click the word *partnerchip* to display the shortcut menu. At the top of the shortcut menu, click **partnership** to correct the misspelling.

More Knowledge | **Checking the Spelling of an Entire Message**

To check the spelling of all the content in the message body at one time, click the Review tab. In the Proofing group, click the Spelling & Grammar button. The Spelling and Grammar dialog box displays the first unrecognized word and suggested corrections. You can proceed through the entire message, correcting each misspelled word. The spelling checker doesn't check spelling in the message header (the recipient fields and message subject).

Activity 1.14 | Modifying Message Settings and Delivery Options

Recall that setting message importance and message sensitivity are options that you can use with messages. You can also set various *message delivery options* that are applied at the time a message is delivered. One of the messages you will send for Darron Jacobsen is of a personal nature, and he also wants to be informed when the recipient has actually read the message.

1 With Darron's message to Lisa still displayed, on the **Message tab**, in the **Tags group**, click **High Importance**.

2 On the **Options tab**, in the **More Options group**, click the **Dialog Box Launcher** 🔹, and then compare your screen with Figure 1.34.

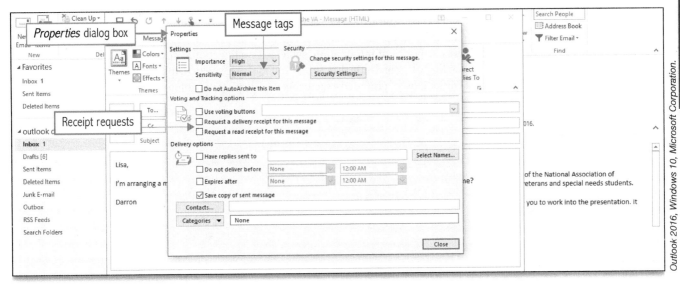

FIGURE 1.34

Outlook 2016, Windows 10, Microsoft Corporation.

3 In the **Properties** dialog box, notice that under **Settings**, **Importance** is set to **High**. Click the **Sensitivity** arrow, and then click **Personal**.

It is good practice to use discretion when discussing confidential or personal information in your email messages. Recall that the privacy of your email messages cannot be guaranteed.

4 Under **Voting and Tracking options**, select the **Request a read receipt for this message** check box.

By selecting this setting, you will be notified when the recipient reads this message.

5 In the lower right corner of the **Properties** dialog box, click **Close**. **Send** the message, click **Add Account**, and then click **Cancel** (or click **Close** ⊠ in the Connect message) to place the message in the **Drafts** folder.

6 In the **Inbox**, locate and select the message from Mary Adair with the subject *Purchase Order* to display it in the **Reading Pane**.

When Mary sent this message, she set the Importance to *High*. In the message list, a High Importance icon displays above the date, and in the Reading Pane, a banner displays in the lower portion of the message header.

More Knowledge | **Displaying Message Properties**

There are multiple ways to display the Properties dialog box for a message. You can also click the Dialog Box Launcher in the Tags group on the Message tab, or display the Info page of the Backstage view and click Properties.

Activity 1.15 | Sorting Inbox Messages

Sometimes you will want to sort your messages by a specific message attribute. For example, you may want to see the messages in order by sender or by subject. As you will see while working with Darron's Inbox, different arrangements expose additional information about messages.

1 On the **View tab**, in the **Layout group**, click **Reading Pane**, and then click **Bottom**. Compare your screen with Figure 1.35.

The Reading Pane displays in the lower portion of the Outlook window, below the message list. When the Reading Pane is turned off or is displayed at the bottom of the Outlook window, you can see the *column headings* above the message list. The column headings identify the message *fields*, which are categories of information, such as the subject of a message or the date and time received. Depending on your Outlook settings, the messages may display differently than the figure. Many Outlook users prefer arrangements that display the column headings.

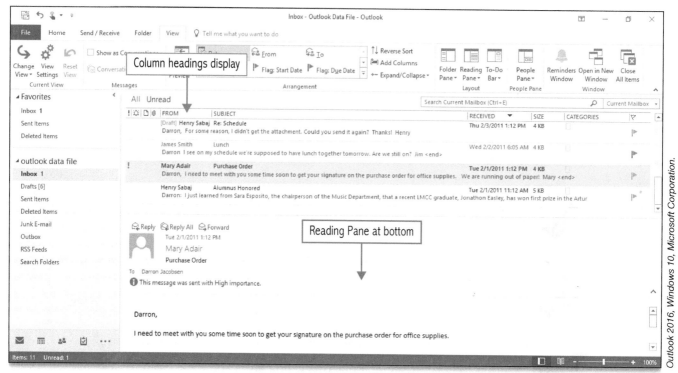

FIGURE 1.35

2 Above the message list, point to the column heading **SUBJECT**, and notice the ScreenTip *Sort by: Subject*.

Use the column headings to sort your messages by field. The field used by default to sort Inbox messages is the *Received* date and time, with the most recent message displayed first. The leftmost column headings are icons for sorting by Importance, by Reminder, by Icon, or by Attachment.

3 Click the **FROM** column heading to sort the messages by that field. Notice that an upward-pointing arrow displays to the right of *FROM*.

The Inbox messages are sorted alphabetically by the sender's first name. The up arrow in the FROM header indicates an ascending sort order—from A to Z.

4 Click the **FROM** column heading again to change the sort order to descending—from Z to A.

The downward-pointing arrow in the From header indicates a descending sort order.

5 Drag the **scroll box** up or down and notice that the messages are grouped by the message sender.

6 Click the **RECEIVED** column heading to restore sorting by the date and time received.

Recall that received messages flow into your Inbox by the date and time received, which is the default sort order.

7 On the **View tab**, in the **Arrangement group**, click the **More** ⊽ button, and then in the displayed gallery of arrangement options, click **Flag: Due Date**. Scroll to the bottom of the message list, and then compare your screen with Figure 1.36.

> The Inbox messages are arranged by due date, with messages that do not have a due date displayed at the top of the list.

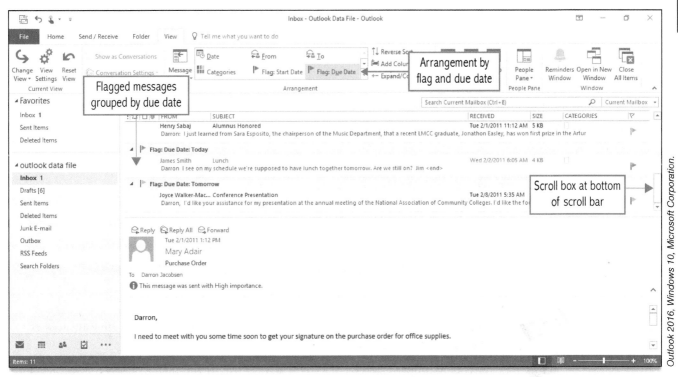

FIGURE 1.36

8 Without changing the Inbox view, start **PowerPoint 2016** and click **Blank Presentation**. If necessary, **Maximize** ☐ the PowerPoint window, and close the Welcome pane if it is open.

9 On the **Home tab**, in the **Slides** group, click **Layout**, and then in the displayed gallery, click **Blank** to change the slide layout of Slide 1.

10 With Slide 1 displayed in PowerPoint, on the **Insert tab**, in the **Images group**, click **Screenshot**, and then under **Available Windows**, click the image of your Outlook window to insert it on the slide. If multiple images display under Available Windows, point to the thumbnail images to display the window titles. Your Outlook window will have the title *Inbox – Outlook Data File - Outlook*.

11 If the Design Ideas pane opens on the right, close it. Click in a white area to deselect the image, and then compare your screen with Figure 1.37.

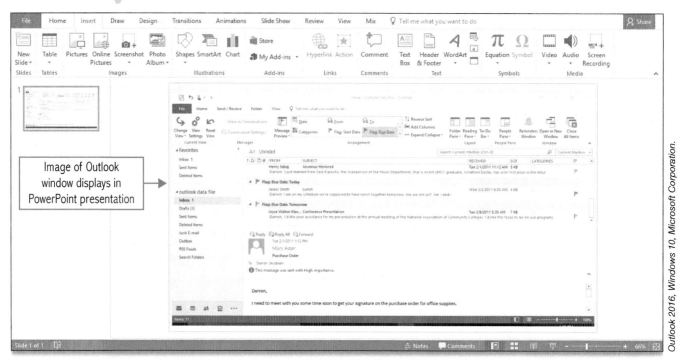

Image of Outlook window displays in PowerPoint presentation

FIGURE 1.37

12 In PowerPoint, click the **File tab**, click **Save As** in the left pane, and then click **Browse** to display the **Save As** dialog box.

13 In the **Save As** dialog box, navigate to the location where you plan to store your Projects for this chapter so that the location displays in the **address bar**. On the toolbar, click **New folder**, type **Outlook Chapter 1** and then press ⏎.

14 In the file list, double-click your **Outlook Chapter 1** folder to open it. Click in the **File name** box, and then, using your own name, replace the selected text by typing **Lastname_Firstname_1A_Outlook** Click **Save**, and then in the upper right corner of the PowerPoint window, click **Minimize** ⏤ so that PowerPoint remains open but is not displayed on your screen.

You will need your PowerPoint presentation again as you progress through this Project.

15 In **Outlook**, on the **View tab**, in the **Arrangement group**, click the **More** ⏷ button, and then in the displayed gallery, click **Attachments**. Scroll to the top of the message list.

The Inbox messages are arranged so that messages that include an attachment are displayed before those that do not.

16 Click the **RECEIVED** column heading to restore the original sort order.

17 On the **View tab**, in the **Layout group**, click **Reading Pane**, and then click **Right** to return the Reading Pane to its default position.

More **Knowledge**   **Changing Column Widths**

When the Reading Pane is displayed in the lower portion of the Outlook screen or is turned off, you can resize the column widths for the list view of any Outlook module. Drag the divider that separates the column headers to the left or right to decrease or increase the column width, or double-click it to adjust the column width to fit its content.

> **More Knowledge** | **Managing Conversations**
>
> A *conversation* is a chain of email messages that stem from the same original message and have the same subject. If a conversation no longer applies to you, you can click Ignore in the Delete group on the Home tab. That moves all current and future messages in the conversation directly to your Deleted Items folder. On the Home tab, in the Delete group, click Clean Up and then click Conversation to delete earlier messages that are included within reply messages. These features are useful when a conversation includes many recipients exchanging messages.

Activity 1.16 | Printing Messages

Recall that Outlook organizes its information in folders. To print information in Outlook, each folder type has one or more predefined print styles associated with it. A *print style* is a combination of page and content settings that determines the way items print. For the Inbox folder, there are two predefined print styles—*Table Style* and *Memo Style*. Memo style is the default print setting and prints the text of selected items as individual printouts. Table Style prints selected items or all the items in a list with the visible columns displayed. In this Activity, you will print Darron's Inbox and Drafts folder messages in the predefined print styles.

1 In the **Inbox**, select the last message in the list—the message from Henry Sabaj with the subject *Alumnus Honored*. Click the **File tab**, and then in the left pane, click **Print**.

2 On the **Print** page, under **Settings**, click **Table Style**. On the right, notice the **Preview** image. Compare your screen with Figure 1.38.

Use Table Style to print a list view of multiple items, such as the contents of a folder.

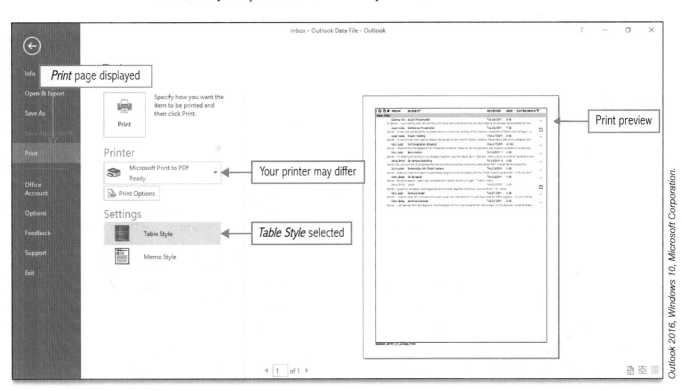

FIGURE 1.38

Outlook 2016, Windows 10, Microsoft Corporation.

3 Under **Printer**, click **Print Options**. In the displayed **Print** dialog box, under **Print style**, click **Page Setup**.

4 In the displayed **Page Setup: Table Style** dialog box, click the **Header/Footer tab**. Under **Footer**, select and delete any existing text from the three white boxes. Then click in the leftmost white box to place the insertion point. Using your own first and last names, type **Lastname_Firstname_1A_College_Inbox** Do not be concerned if your text wraps to another line. Under **Header**, if necessary, delete any existing text from the three boxes. Compare your screen with Figure 1.39.

> Print styles may include the user name, the page number, and the print date in the footer, or they may include other information. If the text you type in the Footer box wraps to two lines, when the page is printed, the footer appears on a single line.

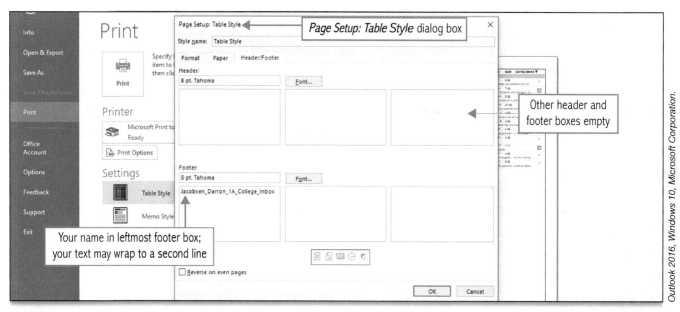

FIGURE 1.39

ALERT! **Does your screen show a different header or footer?**

Outlook remembers previously entered headers and footers. The boxes for this information in the Page Setup dialog box may indicate a previous user's name or some other information. You can enter new information in these boxes and Outlook will retain this information for the next header or footer you print in this print style.

---

5 In the **Page Setup: Table Style** dialog box, click the **Paper tab**. Under **Paper**, click **Letter** if this option is not already selected. Click **OK** to close the dialog box.

> On the Paper tab, you can also control the page size, margins, and orientation of the print output.

6 In the lower right corner of the **Print** dialog box, click **Preview**, and then point to the print preview. Notice that the pointer looks like a magnifying glass. Click the lower left corner of the print preview to zoom in on it, and notice the custom footer you created in Step 4.

7 From the Windows taskbar, open your **Lastname_Firstname_1A_Outlook** PowerPoint presentation. On the **Home tab**, click the **New Slide arrow**, and then click **Blank** to add a new blank slide. With Slide 2 displayed, on the **Insert tab**, in the **Images group**, click **Screenshot**, and then under **Available Windows**, click the image of your Outlook window to insert it on the slide.

8 On the **Quick Access Toolbar**, click **Save** 🖫, and then **Minimize** ⊟ the PowerPoint window.

9 In **Outlook**, in the upper left corner of the **Print** page, click the **Back arrow** ⊙ to return to the **Inbox** without printing the message list. In the **Folder Pane**, click **Drafts** to display this folder, which contains your sent messages.

10 In the **message list**, click the message with the subject *RE: Joyce's Presentation*.

11 From the Windows taskbar, open your **Lastname_Firstname_1A_Outlook** PowerPoint presentation. Insert a new slide in the Blank layout. With Slide 3 displayed, on the **Insert tab**, in the **Images group**, click **Screenshot**, and then click the image of your Outlook window to insert it on the slide.

12 **Save** 🖫 your file, and then **Minimize** ⊟ the PowerPoint window.

13 In Outlook, click the **File tab**, click **Print**, and then be sure **Memo Style** is selected.

> Use Memo Style to print individual items, such as an entire email message.

14 Using the technique you practiced earlier in this Activity, add a footer with your name as **Lastname_Firstname_1A_Drafts** and delete any other headers or footers. In the **Page Setup: Memo Style** dialog box, click **OK**. In the **Print** dialog box, click **Preview**. Then click the upper-left corner of the print preview to zoom in, and notice the follow up flag information.

15 From the Windows taskbar, open your **Lastname_Firstname_1A_Outlook** presentation, and insert a new slide in the Blank layout. With Slide 4 displayed in PowerPoint, on the **Insert tab**, in the **Images group**, click **Screenshot**, and then click the image of your Outlook window.

16 **Save** 🖫 your file, and then **Minimize** ⊟ the PowerPoint window.

17 In **Outlook**, in the upper left corner of the **Print page**, click the **Back arrow** ⊙ to return to your **Drafts** folder without printing the message.

Activity 1.17 | Deleting Messages

After you read and reply to a message, it is good practice to either delete it or store it in another folder for future reference. Doing so keeps your Inbox clear of messages that you have already handled. When you delete a message from your Inbox folder or any other mail folder, it is moved to the Deleted Items folder. Items remain in this folder until you empty the folder, at which time the items are permanently deleted. You can see that this is helpful in case you delete a message by mistake; you can still retrieve it from the Deleted Items folder until that folder is emptied. You can delete messages in a variety of ways—with commands from the ribbon, from the keyboard, or from a menu.

1 Display your **Inbox** folder, and then select the message from Mary Adair with the subject *Some Advice*.

2 On the **Home tab**, in the **Delete group**, click **Delete** to move the message to the **Deleted Items** folder.

> Because the deleted message was marked as Read, the Folder Pane doesn't change to show that the Deleted Items folder contains a message.

3 Select the message from Lisa Huelsman with the subject *Partnership with Illinois Veterans*. Hold down Ctrl, and then click the message from James Smith with the subject *Lunch*. Compare your screen with Figure 1.40.

> Use this technique to select non-adjacent (not next to each other) items in any Windows-based program.

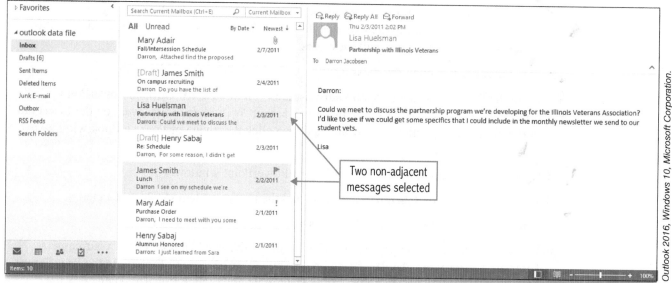

FIGURE 1.40

4 On your keyboard, press [Delete] to delete the selected messages.

5 In the **message list**, click the first message, scroll down ▼ if necessary to display the last message, hold down [Shift], and then click the last message to select the remaining messages.

6 Right-click any of the selected messages to display a shortcut menu of actions you can take with the selected messages. On the shortcut menu, click **Delete**.

The selected messages are deleted, and the message list for the Inbox is empty.

7 In the **Folder Pane**, click **Drafts**. In the **message list**, click any message. Then press [Ctrl] + [A] to select all the messages in the folder. Using one of the techniques you just practiced, delete all the messages.

8 Display the **message list** for the **Deleted Items** folder. Notice that it contains the received and draft messages you deleted.

9 From the Windows taskbar, open your **Lastname_Firstname_1A_Outlook** presentation, and insert a new slide in the blank layout. With Slide 5 displayed in PowerPoint, on the **Insert tab**, in the **Images group**, click **Screenshot**, and then click the image of your Outlook window.

10 Save 🖫 your file, and then **Close** ☒ the PowerPoint window.

11 In the **Folder Pane**, right-click the **Deleted Items** folder, and then on the shortcut menu click **Empty Folder**.

Outlook displays a warning box indicating that you are permanently deleting the selected items.

12 In the **Microsoft Outlook** dialog box, click **Yes** to permanently delete the items and empty the folder.

Activity 1.18 │ Using Outlook Help and Restoring Outlook Email Defaults

As you work with Outlook, you can get assistance by using the Help feature. You can ask questions, and Outlook Help will provide you with information and step-by-step instructions for performing tasks. In this Activity, you will use Outlook Help and restore Outlook's default settings.

1 To the right of the ribbon tabs, click **Tell me what you want to do**, and then type **attachment** Compare your screen with Figure 1.41.

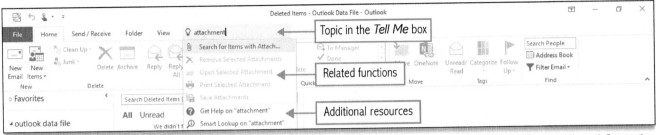

FIGURE 1.41

2 At the bottom of the list, click **Get Help on "attachment"**, and then compare your screen with Figure 1.42.

The entire search string might not be visible in the list. The Outlook Help dialog box displays a list of related Help topics with links in blue text. Clicking these links displays additional information about the topic.

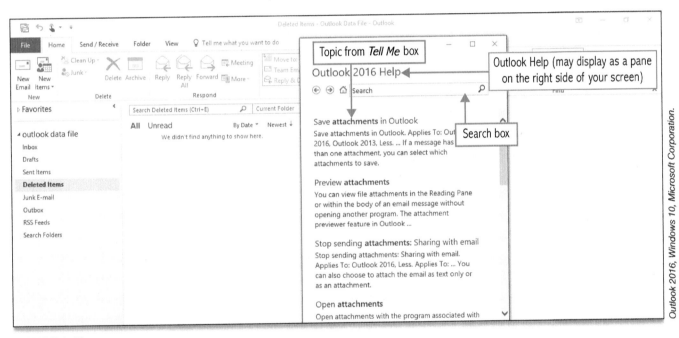

FIGURE 1.42

3 In the list of search results, click **Open attachments**, and then review this information.

4 **Close** ☒ **Outlook Help.**

5 Click the **File tab**, and then click **Options**.

6 In the displayed **Outlook Options** dialog box, click the **Advanced** page tab. Scroll down ▼ as necessary, and then under **Send and receive**, select the **Send immediately when connected** check box. Then, to the right of the check box, click **Send/Receive**.

7 In the **Send/Receive Groups** dialog box, under **Setting for group "All Accounts"**, select the **Include this group in send/receive (F9)** and **Schedule an automatic send/receive every** check boxes. Under **When Outlook is Offline**, select the **Include this group in send/receive (F9)** check box. Click **Close**, and then in the **Outlook Options** dialog box, click **OK**.

This action restores Outlook's default settings, which you changed at the beginning of this Project for instructional purposes.

8 Click the **File tab**, and then click **Exit**.

9 Submit your **Lastname_Firstname_1A_Outlook** PowerPoint presentation to your instructor as directed.

END | You have completed Project 1A

Manage Contact Records, Tasks, and Appointments

PROJECT ACTIVITIES

In Activities 1.19 through 1.25, you will store contact and task information and record appointments in a daily schedule for Shane Washington, Director of Office Operations for Mayor David Parker of Desert Park, Arizona. As you progress through the Project, you will insert screenshots of your Contacts list, To-Do List, and Calendar into a PowerPoint presentation similar to Figure 1.43.

PROJECT FILES

For Project 1B you will need the following file:

o01B_Mayor's_Contacts

You will save your results in a PowerPoint file as:

Lastname_Firstname_1B_Outlook

PROJECT RESULTS

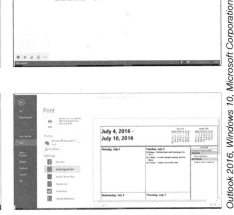

FIGURE 1.43 Project 1B Manage Contact Records, Tasks, and Appointments

Recall that a contact is a person, organization, or business with whom you communicate. A *contact record* contains information such as street and email addresses, telephone and fax numbers, birthdays, and pictures. An *address book* is a folder designated for the storage of contact records. You display and manage address books in Outlook's People module.

Activity 1.19 | Importing Contact Records into Your People Module

In this Activity, you will import contact records and some associated messages into your People module. The imported contact records contain information about various members of the Desert Park city government.

1 Start Outlook 2016, and select the **Profile** you created in **Project 1A**. If you are using a different computer and that Profile is not available, repeat Activity 1.01 on the computer at which you are working and create the Profile.

2 Click the **File tab**, click **Open & Export**, and then click **Import/Export**.

3 In the displayed **Import and Export Wizard** dialog box, under **Choose an action to perform**, click **Import from another program or file**, and then click **Next**.

4 In the **Import a File** dialog box, under **Select file type to import from**, click **Outlook Data File (.pst)**, and then click **Next**.

5 In the **Import Outlook Data File** dialog box, click **Browse**. In the displayed **Open Outlook Data Files** dialog box, navigate to the location where you have stored the student files for this textbook. Locate **o01B_Mayor's_Contacts**, click one time to select it, and then click **Open**.

6 In the **Import Outlook Data File** dialog box, click **Next**, and then click **Finish**.

7 Below the **Folder Pane**, on the **Navigation Bar**, click **People** 👥. If necessary, on the **View tab**, in the **Layout group**, click **Reading Pane**, and then click **Right**. Then, on the ribbon, click the **Home tab** if necessary. Compare your screen with Figure 1.44.

The first contact on the list—Gloria French—is selected, and her *People Card* displays in the Reading Pane on the right. The People Card collects all the important details about a contact in one place: phone, email, address, company information, social media updates, and depending on your connection, whether or not the person is available. From the card, you can initiate contact with the person, in the form of an instant message, phone call, meeting, or email message.

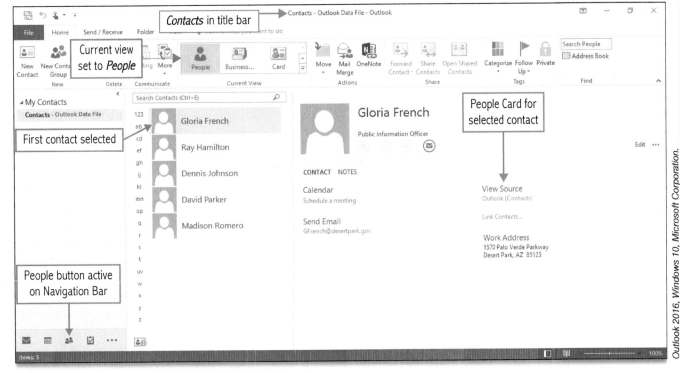

FIGURE 1.44

Activity 1.20 | Creating and Viewing Contacts

When you create a new contact, you add it to your Contacts address book. In this Activity, you will add Shane Washington, Director of Office Operations for the mayor of Desert Park, as a contact.

1 If necessary, click **People** 🔲 on the **Navigation Bar** to display your contacts. In the **Folder Pane**, be sure the **Contacts** folder is selected.

2 On the **Home tab**, in the **New group**, click **New Contact. Maximize** 🔲 the displayed contact form, and then compare your screen with Figure 1.45.

> The Untitled – Contact form displays. You can store a variety of information about a person or an organization on the pages of the contact form. You can use the blank area of the form, referred to as the *Notes area*, for any information about the contact that doesn't have a corresponding form field.

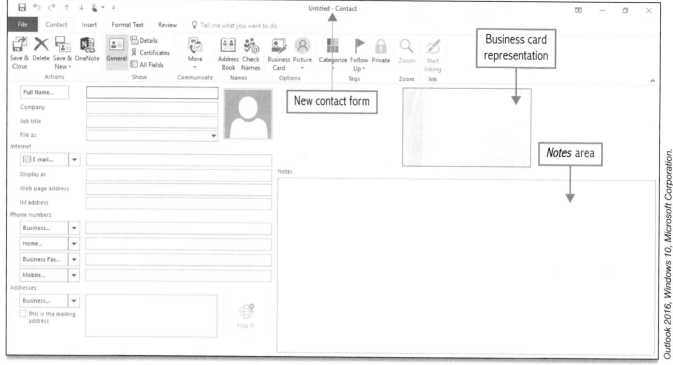

FIGURE 1.45

3 In the **Untitled – Contact** form, in the **Full Name** box, type **Shane Washington** and then press Tab.

The insertion point moves to the Company box, and the form title bar displays *Shane Washington – Contact*. Notice that the *File as* box displays the contact name as *Washington, Shane*. This is how it will appear in the Contacts list. By default, Outlook displays items in the Contacts list in alphabetical order based on last names, a common method for arranging groups of names.

4 In the **Company** box, type **Desert Park Mayor's Office** and then press Tab. In the **Job title** box, type **Director of Office Operations**

On the right side of the contact form, the information you enter displays in a business card format.

5 Click in the **Email** box, type **SWashington@desertpark.gov** and then press Tab.

The Display as box shows the contact's name with the email address in parentheses. When you enter the contact's name or email address in the To or Cc box of an email message, this is how Outlook will display the address. Some contacts will have multiple email addresses, and some email addresses may be completely unrelated to the person's actual name. When viewing email messages, this feature helps you identify the correct email address for the person you want to communicate with.

6 Under **Phone numbers**, in the **Business** box, type **6265550129** and then press Tab. If a Location Information dialog box displays, select your country or region, type your area code, and click OK two times. Compare your screen with Figure 1.46.

Outlook changes the format of the entered phone number to (626) 555-0129.

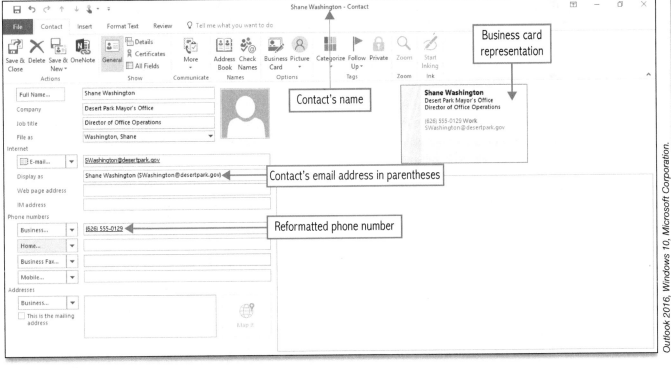

FIGURE 1.46

7 ▶ Under **Addresses**, be sure that Business is shown. If Home or Other is shown, click the adjacent arrow, and then click Business. Click in the **Business** box. Type **1570 Palo Verde Parkway** press Enter, and then type **Desert Park, AZ 85123**

8 ▶ On the contact form ribbon, on the **Contact tab**, in the **Actions group**, click **Save & Close**.

Outlook saves the new contact and the Contacts folder displays the new contact in its correct alphabetical position.

9 ▶ On the **Home tab**, in the **Current View group**, click the More ▾ button, and then in the displayed gallery, click **Business Card**. Compare your screen with Figure 1.47.

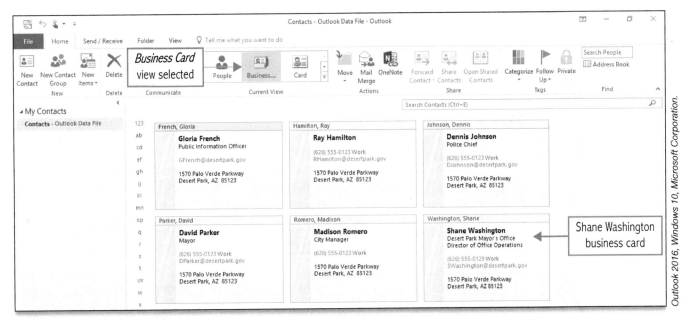

FIGURE 1.47

10 In the lower left corner of the screen, on the **Navigation Bar**, click **Mail** ✉. In the **Folder Pane**, be sure the **Inbox** folder is selected.

> The Inbox contains a message from Simone Daley. This message was imported into your Inbox when you imported the contact records. There is no listing in your Contacts address book for Simone.

11 In the **message list**, point to the text *Simone Daley*, hold down the left mouse button, and then drag the message down to the lower left corner of the screen so that the pointer is over the **People** 👥 button on the **Navigation Bar**. Release the left mouse button when you see + attached to the pointer, and then compare your screen with Figure 1.48.

> A new contact form displays with Simone's name in the title bar, her name and email address in the appropriate form fields, and the text of her email message in the Notes area. If you receive an email message from someone that you would like to put in your Contacts address book, this is a fast way to do so.

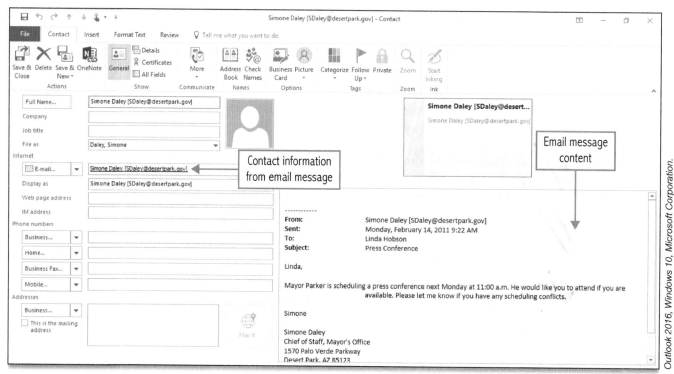

FIGURE 1.48

12 Type the following business phone number and address in the corresponding form fields:

626-555-0128
1570 Palo Verde Parkway
Desert Park, AZ 85123

13 On the **Contact tab**, in the **Actions group**, click **Save & Close**. On the **Navigation Bar**, click the **People** 👥 button, and notice that Simone Daley's contact record is added to the list.

14 Start **PowerPoint 2016** and click **Blank Presentation. Maximize** ☐ the PowerPoint window if it doesn't fill the screen. On the **Home tab**, in the **Slides group**, click **Layout**, and then in the displayed gallery, click **Blank**.

15 With Slide 1 displayed in PowerPoint, on the **Insert tab**, in the **Images group**, click **Screenshot**, and then under **Available Windows**, click the image of your Outlook window to insert it on the slide.

16 In PowerPoint, click the **File tab**, click **Save As**, and then click **Browse**. In the displayed **Save As** dialog box, if necessary, navigate to your **Outlook Chapter 1** folder you created in Project 1A, and open it. Using your own name, replace the text in the **File name** box with **Lastname_Firstname_1B_Outlook** Click **Save**, and then **Minimize** — the PowerPoint window.

You will need your PowerPoint presentation again as you progress through this Project.

Activity 1.21 | Editing and Printing Your Contact List

It is common to create a contact record and then add more information later as it becomes available. Two members of Desert Park's government are new in their positions. In this Activity, you will edit the existing entries by adding more information and then print the entire contact list.

1 In the **Folder Pane**, be sure **Contacts** is selected. On the **Home tab**, in the **Current View group**, click the **More** ☰ button, and then in the displayed gallery, click **People**. Double-click the **Madison Romero** contact to display the People Card view of Ms. Romero's contact record.

The People Card presents a different view of the information than is available in the contact form.

🔄 **ANOTHER WAY**   To open an existing contact record, select the contact and then use the keyboard shortcut Ctrl + O.

2 To the left of **Email**, click ⊕, and then in the displayed **Email** box, type **MRomero@desertpark.gov** In the lower right corner, click **Save**, and then in the upper right corner of Ms. Romero's People Card, click **Close** ✕.

3 In the **Contacts** list, click **Gloria French** to select the contact. In the **Reading Pane**, on the right edge the **People Card**, click **Edit**. To the left of **Phone**, click ⊕, and then click **Work**. In the displayed **Work** box, type **626-555-0123**

4 In the lower right corner, click **Save**, and then compare your screen with Figure 1.49.

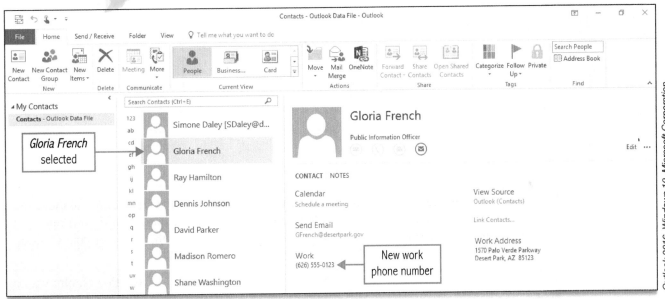

FIGURE 1.49

5 In the contact list, click **Simone Daley**. Press and hold Ctrl and click **Gloria French**, **Madison Romero**, and **Shane Washington** to select the contact records you modified. Then release the Ctrl key.

6 On the ribbon, click the **File tab**, and then click **Print**. Under **Settings**, click each style to see a preview of all the existing contact records as they would be printed in that style.

Each of the different print styles arranges the contact information in a different format. The right pane displays a preview of the existing contact records in the selected print style.

7 Under **Settings**, click **Card Style**, and then under **Printer**, click **Print Options**. In the displayed **Print** dialog box, under **Print range**, click the **Only selected items** option button, and then in the lower right corner of the dialog box, click **Preview**.

The print preview updates to show only the four selected contact records in the Card Style print style.

8 In the lower right corner of the preview area, click the **Actual Size** button. Compare your screen with Figure 1.50.

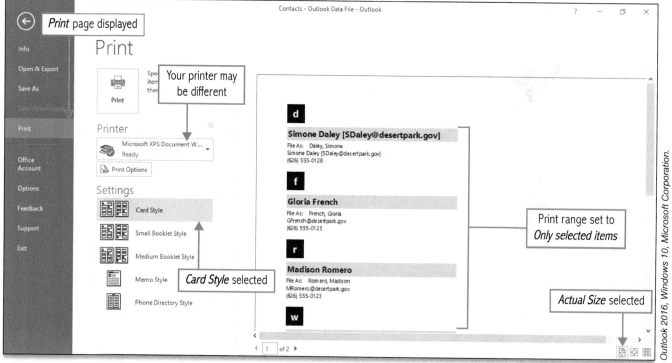

FIGURE 1.50

9 From the Windows taskbar, open your **Lastname_Firstname_1B_Outlook** presentation, and then from the **Home tab**, add a new blank slide. With Slide 2 displayed in PowerPoint, on the **Insert tab**, in the **Images group**, click **Screenshot**, and then click the image of your Outlook window to insert it on the slide.

10 On the **Quick Access Toolbar**, click **Save**, and then **Minimize** your PowerPoint window.

11 In **Outlook**, in the upper left corner of the **Print page**, click the **Back arrow** to return to your **Contacts** folder without printing the contact records.

In Outlook, a **task** is a personal or work-related activity that you want to keep track of until it is complete. For example, writing a report, creating a memo, making a sales call, and organizing a staff meeting are all tasks. You can create tasks for yourself, create tasks and assign them to other people, and accept task assignments from other Outlook users. You display and manage tasks in Outlook's Tasks module.

Activity 1.22 | Creating and Printing a To-Do List

You can create a new task using a New Task form or enter a new task directly in the To-Do List. In this Activity, you will create tasks for Shane Washington.

> **1** In the lower left corner of the screen, on the **Navigation Bar**, click **Tasks** ☑. On the **Home tab**, in the **New group**, click **New Task**. In the **Untitled – Task** form, in the **Subject** box, type **Prepare mayor's Japan travel itinerary**

> **2** In the **Due date** box, click the **Date Picker** 🗔, and then on the displayed calendar, click a date **ten** *business days*—days that are not Saturday, Sunday, or a holiday—from today's date. Compare your screen with Figure 1.51.

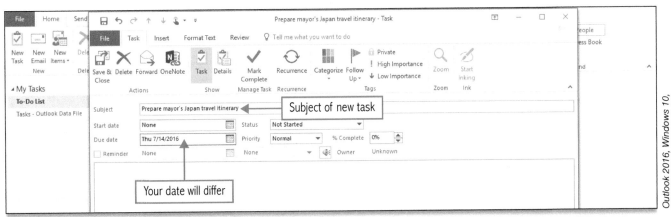

FIGURE 1.51

Outlook 2016, Windows 10, Microsoft Corporation.

> **3** On the **Task tab**, in the **Actions group**, click **Save & Close**. Notice that the **To-Do List** displays the new task.

> **4** On the **Navigation Bar**, click **Mail** ✉. In the **Inbox**, locate the message from Simone Daley with the subject *Press Conference*. Drag the message from the **message list** to the **Tasks** ☑ button on the **Navigation Bar**. Release the left mouse button when you see + attached to the pointer, and then compare your screen with Figure 1.52.

> A new Task form opens containing the information in the email. This is a quick way to add a task generated from an email you received.

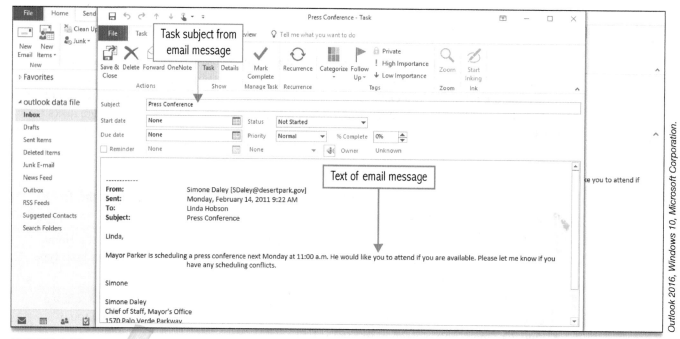

FIGURE 1.52

5 ▶ Set the **Due date** to the Friday following the current date. Click the **Priority arrow**, and then click **High**. In the *task body*—the area in the lower half of the form—click in the blank area above the email text. Type **Complete attendance list for next week's press conference**. Compare your screen with Figure 1.53.

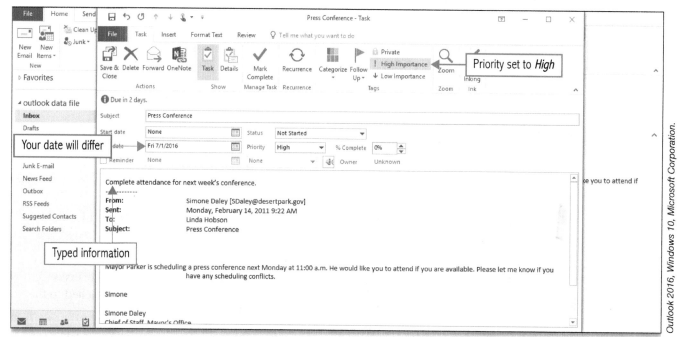

FIGURE 1.53

6 ▶ In the **Actions group**, click **Save & Close**.

7 ▶ On the **Navigation Bar**, click **Tasks** 📋.

8 ▶ From the Windows taskbar, open your **Lastname_Firstname_1B_Outlook** presentation, and insert a new slide in the blank layout. With Slide 3 displayed in PowerPoint, on the **Insert tab**, in the **Images group**, click **Screenshot**, and then click the image of your Outlook window to insert it on the slide.

9 ▸ **Save** 🖫 your presentation, and then **Minimize** ⎯ the PowerPoint window.

10 ▸ On the ribbon, click the **File tab**, and then click **Print**. Notice that only one print style—**Table Style**—is available for printing all tasks.

When one or more tasks are selected, you can print individual tasks in Memo Style.

11 ▸ Under **Printer**, click **Print Options**. In the **Print** dialog box, under **Print style**, click **Page Setup**. In the **Page Setup: Table Style** dialog box, click the **Paper** tab. Under **Orientation**, click the **Landscape** option button. Click **OK**, and then click **Preview**.

12 ▸ In **Outlook**, in the upper left corner of the **Print page**, click the **Back arrow** ⊙ to return to your **To-Do List** without printing it.

Objective 6 | Manage a Calendar

You display and manage your schedule and calendar-related information in Outlook's Calendar module. The default location for Outlook's calendar information is the Calendar folder. To add an item to your calendar, display the folder by clicking the Calendar button on the Navigation Bar.

Activity 1.23 | Exploring the Calendar

In this Activity, you will use the Folder Pane, the Navigation Bar, and the *Date Navigator*—the small calendar displayed in the Folder Pane or in the Calendar peek that provides a quick way to display specific dates or ranges of dates in the calendar. A *peek* is a small window that displays when you point to the Calendar, People, or Tasks button on the Navigation Bar. The peek contains current calendar, contact, or task information that you can interact with.

1 ▸ On the **Navigation Bar**, click **Calendar** ▦. On the **Home tab** of the ribbon, in the **Arrange group**, click **Day**. Compare your screen with Figure 1.54.

The Date Navigator and Folder Pane are on the left side of the screen. To their right is the *appointment area*, which displays the calendar entries in the currently selected time period. An *appointment* is a calendar activity occurring at a specific time to which you do not need to invite other people and for which you do not need to reserve rooms, equipment, or other resources. The date shaded in blue in the Date Navigator and shown at the top of the appointment area is the date that you are viewing, which is, by default, the current date.

On the left and right sides of the appointment area, the Previous Appointment and Next Appointment buttons allow quick movement to days that have scheduled appointments, meetings, or events.

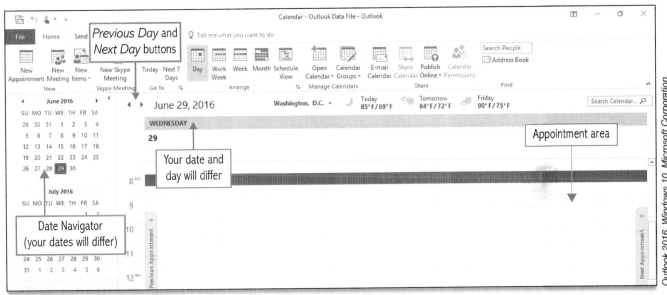

FIGURE 1.54

2 In the **Date Navigator**, click a different day of the month.

The date displayed in the appointment area changes to the day of the month you selected in the Date Navigator. In the Date Navigator, the current date remains shaded in blue, and the selected date is highlighted in light blue.

3 In the **Date Navigator**, to the left of the current month name, click the **left arrow**.

The Date Navigator displays the preceding month, and the appointment area displays the same day of that month.

4 In the **Date Navigator**, to the right of the current month name, click the **right arrow** three times to move forward in the calendar three months.

The Date Navigator displays future months, and the appointment area displays the same day of those months.

5 On the **Home tab**, in the **Arrange group**, click **Week**, notice the data shown, click **Work Week**, and then click **Month**.

The *Week arrangement* displays the seven-day week surrounding the currently displayed day. The *Work Week arrangement* shows only the weekdays, Monday through Friday. The *Month arrangement* shows the calendar month.

6 On the **Home tab**, in the **Go To group**, click **Today** to return to the current day, and then in the **Arrange group**, click **Day**.

7 Click the **Folder tab.** In the **New group**, click **New Calendar**.

8 In the displayed **Create New Folder** dialog box, in the **Name** box, type **Personal Calendar** and then compare your screen with Figure 1.55.

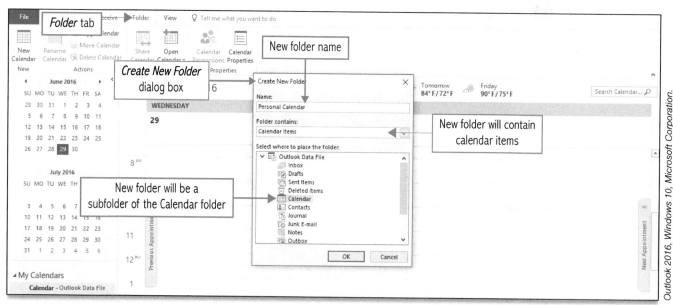

FIGURE 1.55

9 In the **Create New Folder** dialog box, click **OK**.

10 In the **Folder Pane**, under **My Calendars**, select the **Personal Calendar** check box, and then compare your screen with Figure 1.56.

The appointment area splits into two sections, showing both the *Calendar* and the *Personal Calendar*. The calendars are different colors to help you distinguish between appointments on different calendars. If you use more than one calendar, you can display both at the same time.

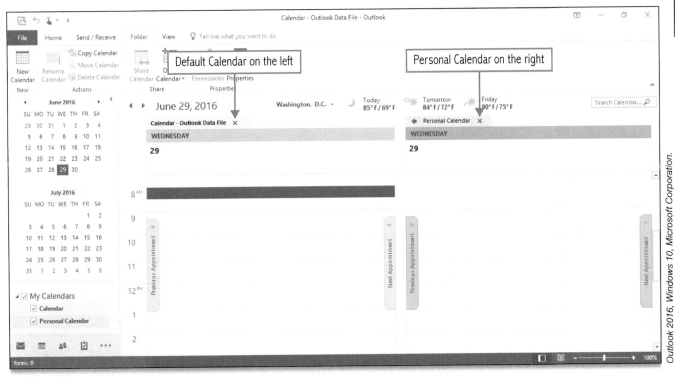

FIGURE 1.56

11 From the Windows taskbar, open your **Lastname_Firstname_1B_Outlook** presentation, and create a new blank slide. With Slide 4 displayed in PowerPoint, on the **Insert tab**, in the **Images group**, click **Screenshot**, and then click the image of your Outlook window to insert it on the slide.

12 Save 💾 your presentation, and then **Minimize** ⊟ the PowerPoint window.

13 In the **Folder Pane**, clear the **Calendar** check box to display only the **Personal Calendar**.

Activity 1.24 | Scheduling Appointments

In Outlook, an appointment occurs at a specific time, for a specific period of time, and does not involve other people or resources. You can create a new appointment directly in the calendar by typing it in a blank time slot in the appointment area. In this Activity, you will schedule appointments in the Personal Calendar for Shane Washington.

1 In the **Date Navigator**, click the **right arrow** one time, advancing the calendar to the next month, and then click the **Tuesday** of the first full week of the displayed month.

The selected date displays at the top of the appointment area, above TUESDAY, which is shaded to match the Personal Calendar color.

2 ▸ Scroll the appointment area as necessary, and click the upper half of the **11 AM** time slot. Type **Weekly meeting with the Mayor** and notice that as you type, the time slot is shaded to match the calendar color and has a black border. Compare your screen with Figure 1.57.

The appointment is scheduled from 11:00 to 11:30. When you use this method to enter an appointment, the default appointment length is 30 minutes.

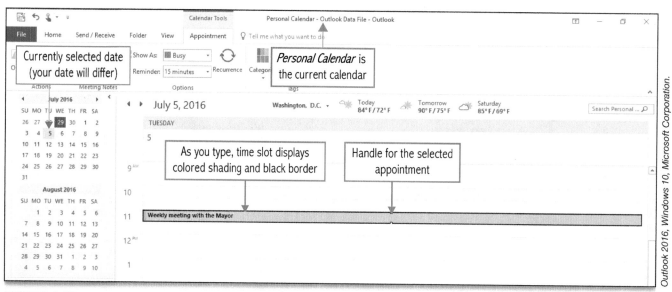

FIGURE 1.57

3 ▸ In the appointment area, click the **12:30 PM** time slot—the lower half of the 12 PM time slot—to enter an appointment on the half hour.

4 ▸ Type **Lunch with Linda** Point to the handle on the bottom of the shaded appointment and when the ⬍ pointer displays, drag the appointment end time down one slot to 1:30 PM. Click any other time slot in the appointment area to deselect, and then compare your screen with Figure 1.58.

The appointment is scheduled from 12:30 to 1:30.

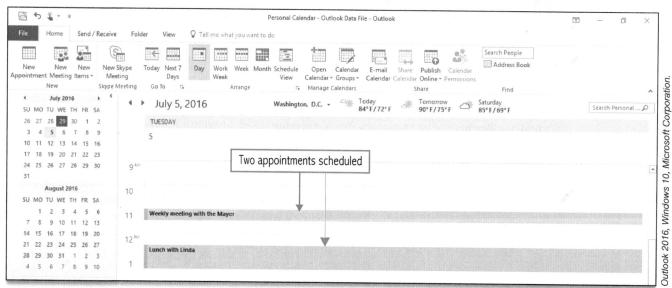

FIGURE 1.58

5 On the **Home tab**, in the **New group**, click **New Appointment**.

The Untitled - Appointment form displays. You can store a variety of information about an appointment, including its subject, location, starting time, and ending time. Notice that the starting and ending times for the new appointment default to those of the time period you clicked in the appointment area. In the **appointment body** in the lower half of the form, you can enter information about the appointment that doesn't match the form fields.

6 As the **Subject** of the appointment, type **Meet with Dominique** In the **Location** box, type **My office**

7 In the right **Start time** box, click the **time arrow**, and then locate and click **9:00 AM**. In the right **End time** box, click the **time arrow**, and then locate and click **10:00 AM (1 hour)**.

8 On the **Appointment tab**, in the **Options group**, click the **Reminder arrow** [Reminder: 15 minutes ▾] and then click **30 minutes**. Compare your screen with Figure 1.59.

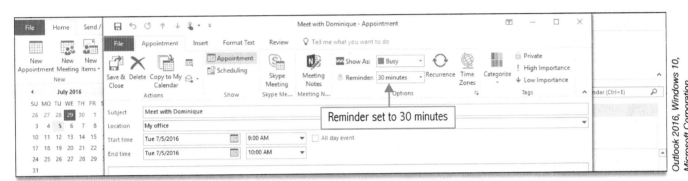

Outlook 2016, Windows 10, Microsoft Corporation.

FIGURE 1.59

9 In the **Actions group**, click **Save & Close**.

The new appointment is added to the calendar. The appointment occupies the 9:00 to 10:00 AM time slot, and the location of the appointment displays below the subject.

10 From the Windows taskbar, open your **Lastname_Firstname_1B_Outlook** presentation, and create a new slide in the blank layout. With Slide 5 displayed in PowerPoint, on the **Insert tab**, in the **Images group**, click **Screenshot**, and then click the image of your Outlook window to insert it on the slide.

11 Save [💾] your presentation, and then **Minimize** [−] the PowerPoint window.

Activity 1.25 │ Printing a Calendar

Depending on what you want to print in your calendar, Outlook has a variety of print styles. You can print a range of hours, a day, a week, or a month. You can also print an individual appointment, event, or meeting invitation.

1 In the **Date Navigator**, click the **Wednesday** of the week in which you have been entering appointments.

2 Click the **File tab**, and then click **Print**. Under **Settings**, click each print style and notice how it displays the calendar information.

Each print style arranges calendar information in a different format. You can preview how the information will display when you print it.

3 Under **Settings**, click **Weekly Agenda Style**. Under **Printer**, click **Print Options**. In the **Print** dialog box, under **Print style**, click **Page Setup**.

4 In the **Page Setup: Weekly Agenda Style** dialog box, on the **Format tab**, under **Options**, click the **Tasks** arrow, and then click **To-Do List**. Select the **Only Print Workdays** check box, and then compare your screen with Figure 1.60.

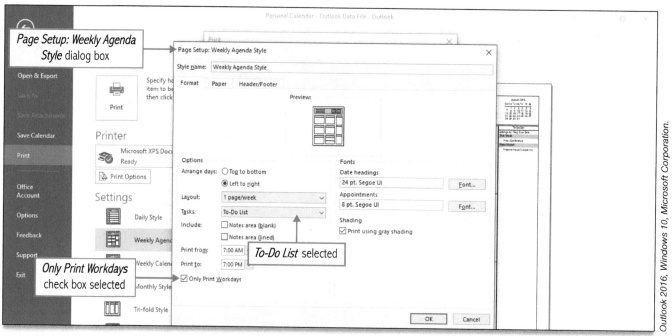

FIGURE 1.60

5 Click **OK**, click **Preview**, and then click the top of the print preview to zoom in on it.

6 From the Windows taskbar, open your **Lastname_Firstname_1B_Outlook** presentation, and create a new slide in the blank layout. With Slide 6 displayed in PowerPoint, on the **Insert tab**, in the **Images group**, click **Screenshot**, and then under **Available Windows**, click the image of your Outlook window to insert it on the slide.

7 **Save** 💾 your presentation, and then **Close** ✕ the PowerPoint window.

8 On the **Print** page, in the upper left corner, click **Back** ⬅ to return to the Personal Calendar without printing it.

9 On the **Navigation Bar**, click **Mail** 📧. Select the email message from Simone Daley, and then on the **Home tab**, in the **Delete group**, click **Delete**.

10 On the **Navigation Bar**, click **People** 👥. With the first contact selected—*Simone Daley*—hold down Shift and click the last contact, *Shane Washington*. Then press Delete to delete all the contact records.

11 On the **Navigation Bar**, click the **Tasks** ☑ button. Press Ctrl + A to select all the tasks, and then press Delete. Click **OK** in the displayed message box to delete the tasks.

12 On the **Navigation Bar**, click **Calendar** ▦. In the **Folder Pane**, right-click **Personal Calendar**, and then on the shortcut menu, click **Delete Calendar**. When the message *Move "Personal Calendar" to your Deleted Items folder* displays, click **Yes**.

13 On the **Navigation Bar**, click **Mail** 📧. In the **Folder Pane**, right-click the **Deleted Items** folder, click **Empty Folder**, and then click **Yes** to permanently delete the items.

14 **Close** ✕ Outlook. Submit your **Lastname_Firstname_1B_Outlook** PowerPoint presentation to your instructor as directed.

Outlook 2016, Windows 10, Microsoft Corporation.

In previous Activities in this textbook, you used Outlook functionality without configuring Outlook to connect to an email account. You can use Outlook to manage messages and information for organization email addresses and for personal email addresses.

You can also use Windows Mail, an app that is built in to Windows 10, to manage email. For your personal email, you may not need all of the features in Outlook 2016, and instead, find that Windows Mail is efficient for managing multiple personal email accounts.

ALERT!   **This Activity is Optional**

This Activity is optional if you would like to create a free Outlook.com email account for personal use.

Activity 1.26 | Create an Outlook.com Email Account

In this Activity, you will create a free Outlook.com email account. Outlook.com is a free email service from Microsoft. It was formerly called *Hotmail* and *Live Mail*. Outlook.com has a web-based interface that is similar to the Outlook user interface. You can access an Outlook.com email account through a web browser, or by connecting to it from an email program such as Outlook or Windows Mail.

Your free Outlook.com email address includes the use of the web-based Microsoft Office Online apps such as Word Online, PowerPoint Online, Excel Online, and OneNote Online. These free online versions do not have all the features of the Microsoft Office software programs, but they are rich in features, and you can use them to read, create, and edit Microsoft Office files.

Do not confuse Outlook.com with the Outlook program—they are not the same.

1 Think about variations of your name that you could use for a professional email address. Consult your instructor for advice if necessary.

> This email address should NOT include any words other than your name, your name with initials, or your name and a number. For example, george_washington@outlook.com, g_washington@outlook.com, or george_washington001@outlook.com. Your first choice for an Outlook.com email address might not be available, so prepare to be flexible.

2 If you already have an Outlook.com account, skip to step 4. If you don't have an Outlook.com account, go to **www.outlook.com** and click **Sign up now**. Follow the instructions to create your account, using only variations of your name and initials with numbers. Be sure to write down your email address and password for later reference.

> This is going to be a professional email address you might use for resumes and for responding to job postings—so no cute or funny words and no nicknames. You will want to maintain this account as your professional email address, and use whatever other email address you have for emailing friends and family members.

3 From the Outlook.com site, open a new message window. Notice the similarities and differences between the Outlook.com email message window and the Outlook email message window.

4 In the **To** box, enter your instructor's email address. In the **Subject** box, enter **My Microsoft Account** In the message body, enter **This is my Microsoft** outlook.com **email address**. Press Enter two times, and type your name. Then send the message.

Activity 1.27 | Use the Windows Mail App

In this Activity, you will start the Windows Mail app and configure it to connect to the email account you created in Activity 1.26.

1 On the Windows taskbar, click in the search box, type **mail** and then in the list of search results, click **Mail Trusted Windows Store app** to start the Mail app.

2 On the displayed **Welcome** screen, click **Get started**. On the **Accounts** screen, click **+ Add account**.

3 In the displayed **Add an account** dialog box, under **Choose an account**, click Outlook.com.

4 On the displayed **Add your Microsoft account** screen, in the **Email or phone** box, enter the Outlook.com email address you created in Activity 1.26. In the **Password** box, enter the password for the Outlook.com email account. Compare your screen with Figure 1.61.

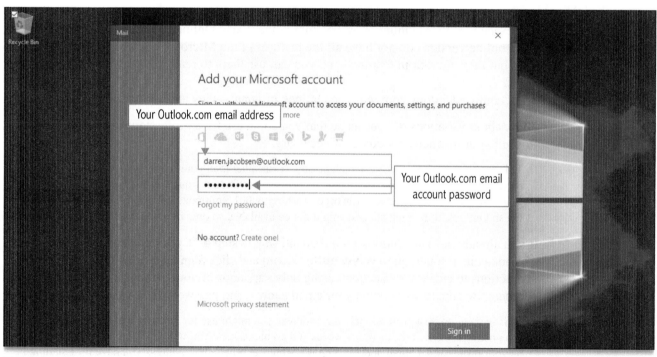

FIGURE 1.61

5 On the **Add your Microsoft account** screen, click **Sign in**. Then compare your screen with Figure 1.62.

FIGURE 1.62

6 On the **Add an account** screen, click **Done**. Then on the **Accounts** screen, click **Ready to go**. Compare your screen with Figure 1.63.

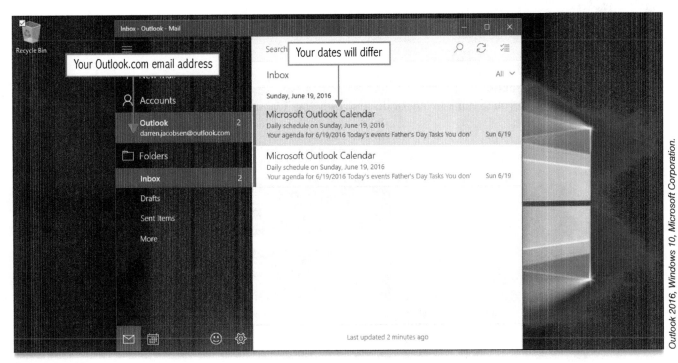

FIGURE 1.63

7 **Close** ☒ all open windows.

END | You have completed Project 1B

END OF CHAPTER

SUMMARY

Job success depends on communicating with others and managing your time, and Outlook is the tool to help you do that. Many professionals in business depend on Outlook and use it many times every day.

One of the most common uses of the personal computer is to send and receive email. Email is the most frequently used way to communicate with coworkers, business contacts, friends, and family members.

By using the modules Mail, Calendar, People, and Tasks, Outlook combines the features of a personal information manager with email capabilities that you can use with other programs within Microsoft Office.

When you set up Outlook, an Outlook Data File is created for each email account. Your email and personal information is stored in folders, and there are separate folders for each of Outlook's modules.

GO! LEARN IT ONLINE

Review the concepts and key terms in this chapter by completing this online challenge.

Matching and Multiple Choice:
Answer matching and multiple choice questions to test what you learned in this chapter.

GO! FOR JOB SUCCESS

Discussion: Email Etiquette

Your instructor may ask you to think about, or discuss with your classmates, these questions:

FotoEdhar/Fotolia

Question 1: Why do you think it is important to follow specific etiquette when composing email?

Question 2: Why is it important to include a greeting and signature in every email that you send?

Question 3: What are the differences between sending a business email and a personal email?

PROJECT GUIDE FOR OUTLOOK 2016 GETTING STARTED

Your instructor may assign one or more of these Projects to help you review the chapter and assess your mastery and understanding of the chapter.

		Project for Outlook 2016 Getting Started Chapter 1	
Project	**Apply Skills from These Chapter Objectives**	**Project Type**	**Project Location**
1A	Objectives 1-3 from Project 1A	**1A Instructional Project (Scorecard Grading)** Guided instruction to learn skills in Project 1A.	In text
1B	Objectives 4-7 from Project 1B	**1B Instructional Project (Scorecard Grading)** Guided instruction to learn skills in Project 1B.	In text
1C	Objectives 1-3 from Project 1A	**1C Mastery (Scorecard Grading) Mastery and Transfer of Learning** A demonstration of your mastery of the skills in Project 1A with decision-making.	In text
1D	Objectives 4-6 from Project 1B	**1D Mastery (Scorecard Grading) Mastery and Transfer of Learning** A demonstration of your mastery of the skills in Project 1B with decision-making.	In text
1E	Combination of Objectives from Projects 1A and 1B	**1E GO! Think (Rubric Grading) Critical Thinking** A demonstration of your understanding of the Chapter concepts applied in a manner that you would use outside of college. An analytic rubric helps you and your instructor grade the quality of your work by comparing it to the work an expert in the discipline would create.	In text
1F	Combination of Objectives from Projects 1A and 1B	**1F GO! Think (Rubric Grading) Critical Thinking** A demonstration of your understanding of the Chapter concepts applied in a manner that you would use outside of college. An analytic rubric helps you and your instructor grade the quality of your work by comparing it to the work an expert in the discipline would create.	In text

GLOSSARY

GLOSSARY OF KEY TERMS

Address book An Outlook folder designated for the storage of contact records.

Appointment A calendar activity occurring at a specific time and day that does not require inviting people or reservations.

Appointment area An area of the Calendar module that displays calendar entries for the currently selected time period.

At sign @ A symbol used to separate the two parts of an email address.

Attachment A separate file that is included with an email message, such as a Word file, a spreadsheet file or an image file.

AutoComplete The Outlook feature that assists you in typing addresses by suggesting previously typed addresses based on the first character you type.

Business day A day other than a Saturday, Sunday, or holiday.

Calendar module A component of Outlook that stores your schedule and calendar-related information.

Column heading Text that identifies message fields.

Contact A person, organization, or business with whom you communicate.

Contact record An Outlook item that contains information about a contact, such as street and email addresses, telephone and fax numbers, birthdays, and a picture.

Conversation A chain of email messages that originate from the same original message and have the same Subject.

Courtesy copy Represented by the letters Cc, a copy of an email.

Credentials A user name or email address and the associated password that provides permission to sign in to an account.

Date Navigator A monthly view of the calendar used to display specific days in a month.

Domain name The second part of an email address, which identifies the host name of the recipient's mail server.

Draft A temporary copy of a message that has not yet been sent.

Favorites Pane An area at the top of the Folder Pane in the Mail module that provides quick access to your primary Inbox and Sent Items folders and any other folders you want to add to it.

Field A category of information within an Outlook item, such as the subject of a message, the date and time received, or a company name or address.

File tab Displays Backstage view, a centralized space for all of your file management tasks such as opening, saving, or printing—all the things you can do *with* a file.

Flagging Marking a message with a flag to draw attention to the message.

Folder Pane Displays in every Outlook module—Mail, Calendar, People, and Tasks—to display folders related to the module.

Formatting text The process of changing the appearance of the text in a message.

Forwarding Sending an email message you have received to someone who did not originally receive it.

Importance Marks that are applied to messages based on the urgency of the message—for example, information that should be read immediately or information that can be read later.

Import The action of bringing existing information into Outlook from another program.

Inbox The folder that stores received email messages.

Mail module A component in Outlook that manages your messages.

Mail profile The Outlook feature that identifies which email account you use and where the related data is stored.

Memo Style A style that prints the text of the selected items one at a time.

Message delivery options Optional settings for an email message that can include the time a message should be sent or the address that should be used for replies.

Message Header The basic information about an email message such as the sender's name, the date sent, and the subject.

Message list area Located to the right of the Folder Pane in the Mail module, the area that displays your mail messages.

Microsoft account A personal or business email account that acts as a single login account for Microsoft systems and services.

Month arrangement A calendar arrangement view that shows the four-, five-, or six-week period that includes the full month.

Navigation Bar Displays navigation controls for each of the main views (modules) in Outlook—Mail, Calendar, People, and Tasks—at the bottom of the Outlook window.

Notes area A blank area of a form in which you can enter any type of information and apply text formatting.

Offline A computer connection status in which the computer is not connected to your organization's network or to the public Internet.

Online A computer connection status in which the computer is connected to your organization's network or to the public Internet.

Outlook Today A single screen that summarizes the day's calendar events and scheduled tasks associated with an email account. You display the Outlook Today view of an account by clicking the account header in the Folder Pane.

Peek A small calendar that displays when you point to the inactive Calendar, People, or Tasks button on the Navigation Bar. The peek contains current calendar, contact, or task information that you can interact with. You can pin a peek to the right side of the Outlook program window.

People Card Collects all the important details about a contact in one place: phone, email, address, company information, social media updates, and depending on your connection, whether or not the person is available. From the card, you can schedule a meeting, send an instant message, or call the person.

People module A component in Outlook that displays and manages your contacts—individuals about whom you have information such as their address, email address, phone numbers, and URLs.

Personal Information Manager A program that enables you to store information about your contacts in electronic form.

Print style A combination of paper and page settings that determines the way Outlook items print.

Quick Access Toolbar Displays buttons to perform frequently used commands with a single click. The default commands include Send/Receive All Folders and Undo. You can add and delete buttons to customize the Quick Access Toolbar for your convenience.

RE: A prefix added to a reply that is commonly used in correspondence to mean *regarding* or *in regard to*.

Reading Pane Displays a preview of a message, located on the right side of the screen.

Ribbon Display Options A button for controlling the display of the ribbon tabs and commands.

Ribbon Displays a group of task-oriented tabs that contain the commands, styles, and resources you need to work in Outlook. The look of your ribbon depends on your screen resolution. A high resolution will display more individual items and button names on the ribbon.

Ribbon group A named set of commands that are related to a specific type of object, item, or action.

Ribbon tab A named page of the ribbon that displays groups of commands related to specific tasks.

Selecting text Highlighting areas of text by dragging with the mouse.

Sensitivity A security label applied to messages that should not be read by others because of the message content.

Status bar The area at the bottom of the Outlook program window that displays and provides access to information about items in the current view, reminders, group notifications, view shortcuts, and zoom controls.

Syntax The way in which the parts of an email address are put together.

Table Style A style that prints multiple items in a list with the visible columns displayed, such as the contents of the Inbox.

Task A personal or work-related activity that you want to keep track of until it is complete.

Task body The blank area in the lower half of the task form in which you can add information not otherwise specified in the form.

Tasks module A component in Outlook that displays and manages your tasks.

Tell Me box A box to the right of the ribbon tabs in which you can enter search terms to find related Outlook commands, Outlook Help articles, and online search results.

Title bar Displays the name of the program and the program window control buttons—Minimize, Maximize/ Restore Down, and Close.

Views Ways to look at similar information in different formats and arrangements.

Week arrangement A calendar arrangement view that shows the seven-day week.

Wizard A tool that walks you through a process in a step-by-step manner.

Work Week arrangement A calendar arrangement view that shows only the weekdays, Monday through Friday.

Zoom button A button that displays the current level of magnification. Clicking the button opens the Zoom dialog box, in which you can specify a magnification level as a percentage or in relation to the page content.

Zoom slider A slider that you drag to changes the level of magnification of on-screen content.

Apply 1A skills from
these Objectives:

1 Start and Navigate
Outlook

2 Send and Receive Email

3 Manage Email

Mastering Outlook Project 1C Enrollment Inbox

In the following Project, you will reply to email messages for Lisa Huelsman of Lake Michigan City College and set up the contents of your Drafts folder to print in Table Style. As you progress through this Project, you will insert screenshots of the results into a PowerPoint presentation similar to Figure 1.64.

 PROJECT FILES

For Project 1C, you will need the following files:

o01C_Enrollments_Inbox
o01C_Enrollments_Schedule

You will save your results in a PowerPoint file as:

Lastname_Firstname_1C_Outlook

PROJECT RESULTS

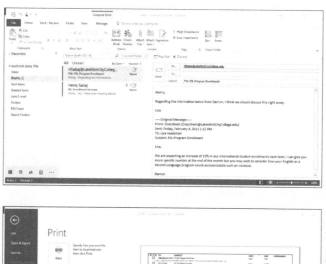

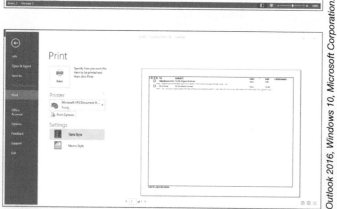

Outlook 2016, Windows 10, Microsoft Corporation.

FIGURE 1.64

(Project 1C Enrollment Inbox continues on the next page)

1 Sign in to Windows, start Outlook 2016, and open the Profile that you created for the Projects in this textbook.

2 Click the **File tab**, click **Options**, and then in the **Outlook Options** dialog box, click the **Advanced** page tab.

3 Scroll down to the **Send and receive** section, clear the **Send immediately when connected** check box, and then on the right, click **Send/Receive**.

4 In the **Send/Receive Groups** dialog box, under **Setting for group "All Accounts"**, clear the **Include this group in send/receive (F9)** and **Schedule an automatic send/receive every** check boxes.

5 Under **When Outlook is Offline**, clear the **Include this group in send/receive (F9)** check box.

6 Click **Close**, and then in the **Outlook Options** dialog box, click **OK** to close the dialog box.

7 On the **Navigation Bar**, click the **Mail** button. If the **Inbox** folder and the **Drafts** folder contain any items, delete those items.

8 Click the **File tab**, click **Open & Export**, and then click **Import/Export**. In the displayed **Import and Export Wizard** dialog box, under **Choose an action to perform**, click **Import from another program or file**, and then click **Next**.

9 In the **Import a File** dialog box, under **Select file type to import from**, click **Outlook Data File (.pst)**, and then click **Next**.

10 In the **Import Outlook Data File** dialog box, click **Browse**. In the **Open Outlook Data Files** dialog box, navigate to the location where the student files for this textbook are stored. Locate **o01C_Enrollments_Inbox**, click it one time to select it, and then click **Open**.

11 Click **Next**, and then click **Finish**. Click your **Inbox** to select its folder, and notice that your **message list** displays two email messages.

12 In the **message list**, double-click the *Enrollment Increase* message to open it in a message window. On the **Message tab**, in the **Respond group**, click **Reply**. With the insertion point at the top of the message body (above the original message), type **Henry,** and then press Enter two times. Type **Yes, I have been hearing about this trend and have some thoughts about it. I can meet with you any day next week. Let me know what time is good for you. I am copying Darron on this reply in case he feels he should be involved in our discussion. I am also including a copy of the Winter/Spring schedule.** Press Enter two times, and then type **Lisa**

13 On the **Message tab**, in the **Include group**, click **Attach File**. In the **Insert File** dialog box, navigate to the student files that accompany this textbook, click **o01C_Enrollments_Schedule**, and then click **Insert**.

14 In the **Tags group**, mark the message with the **High Importance** tag and set the **Follow Up** flag for **Tomorrow**. In the **Tags group**, click the **Dialog Box Launcher** ⌐, and then set the **Sensitivity** to **Confidential**. **Close** the **Properties** dialog box.

15 Click **Send**, click **Add Account**, and then click **Cancel** to store the message in your **Drafts** folder. (Or, if the Connect Outlook to Office 365 window displays, close it.) **Close** ☒ the original message.

(Project 1C Enrollment Inbox continues on the next page)

16 Click the *ESL Program Enrollment* message on time to display it in the **Reading Pane**, and then **Forward** the message to **HSabaj@LakeMichCityCollege.edu** In the message area, click to position the insertion point above the original message, type **Henry,** and then press Enter two times. Type **Regarding the information below from Darron, I think we should discuss this right away.** Press Enter two times, and then type **Lisa**

17 Click **Send**, click **Add Account**, and then click **Cancel** to save the message in your **Drafts** folder. (Or, if the Connect Outlook to Office 365 window displays, close it.)

18 In the **Folder Pane**, click to select your **Drafts** folder so that your reply messages display in the message list.

19 Start **PowerPoint 2016** and click **Blank Presentation**. On the **Home tab**, in the **Slides** group, click **Layout**, and then in the displayed gallery, click **Blank**.

20 With Slide 1 displayed in PowerPoint, on the **Insert tab**, in the **Images group**, click **Screenshot**, and then under **Available Windows**, click the image of your Outlook window to insert it on the slide.

21 In PowerPoint, click the **File tab**, click **Save As**, and then click **Browse**. In the displayed **Save As** dialog box, if necessary, navigate to your **Outlook Chapter 1** folder and open it. Click in the **File name** box, and then, using your own name, replace the selected text by typing **Lastname_Firstname_1C_Outlook** Click **Save**, and then **Minimize** ⊟ the PowerPoint window.

22 Click the **File tab**, and then click **Print**. Under **Settings**, click **Table Style**. Under **Printer**, click **Print Options**. In the **Print** dialog box, under **Print style**, click **Page Setup**.

23 In the **Page Setup: Table Style** dialog box, click the **Header/Footer tab**. Under **Footer**, click in the leftmost white box to place the insertion point. Delete any existing text. Using your own first and last name, type **Lastname_Firstname_1C_Email_Replies** Do not be concerned if your text wraps to another line. Delete any existing information from the center and right footer boxes, and from the three header boxes.

24 In the **Page Setup: Table Style** dialog box, click the **Paper tab**. Under **Orientation**, click **Landscape** if this option is not already selected. Then click **OK**.

25 At the bottom of the **Print** dialog box, click **Preview** to return to the **Print** page. Click the lower left corner of the print preview to zoom in, and notice the footer with your name. Then click again to zoom out.

26 From the Windows taskbar, display your **Lastname_Firstname_1C_Outlook** presentation, and create a new slide in the blank layout. With Slide 2 displayed in PowerPoint, on the **Insert tab**, in the **Images group**, click **Screenshot**, and then under **Available Windows**, click the image of your Outlook window to insert it on the slide.

27 **Save** 🖫 your presentation, and then **Close** ✕ the PowerPoint window.

28 On the **Print** page, click the **Back** button to return to the **Drafts** folder without printing.

29 Delete the contents of the **Drafts** folder and the **Inbox** folder, and then empty the **Deleted Items** folder.

30 Click the **File tab**, and then click **Options**. In the **Outlook Options** dialog box, click the **Advanced** page tab. Scroll down to the **Send and receive** section, select the **Send immediately when connected** check box, and then to its right, click **Send/Receive**.

(Project 1C Enrollment Inbox continues on the next page)

31 In the **Send/Receive Groups** dialog box, under **Setting for group "All Accounts"**, select the **Include this group in send/receive (F9)** and **Schedule an automatic send/receive every** check boxes. Under **When Outlook is Offline**, select the **Include this group in send/receive (F9)** check box. Click **Close** and then click **OK**.

32 Click the **File tab**, and then click **Exit**. Submit your **Lastname_Firstname_1C_Outlook** PowerPoint presentation to your instructor as directed.

END | You have completed Project 1C

Mastering Outlook Project 1D Contacts, Tasks, and Appointments

In the following Project, you will work with contact records, tasks, and appointments related to an upcoming Job Fair. As you progress through the Project, you will insert screenshots of the results into a PowerPoint presentation similar to Figure 1.65.

 PROJECT FILES

For Project 1D, you will need the following file:

o01D_Job_Fair_Contacts

You will save your results in a PowerPoint file as:

Lastname_Firstname_1D_Outlook

PROJECT RESULTS

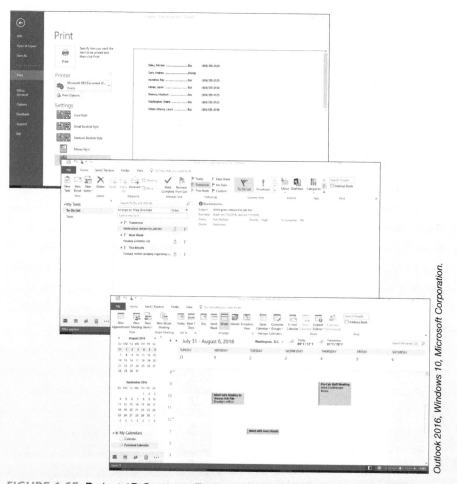

FIGURE 1.65 Project 1D Contacts, Tasks, and Appointments

Outlook 2016, Windows 10, Microsoft Corporation.

(Project 1D Contacts, Tasks, and Appointments continues on the next page)

Mastering Outlook | **Project 1D Contacts, Tasks, and Appointments** (continued)

1 Sign in to Windows, start Outlook 2016, and open the Profile that you created for the Projects in this textbook. Delete any existing items from the People module, and delete any calendars other than the default calendar from the Calendar module.

2 Click the **File tab**, click **Open & Export**, and then click **Import/Export**. In the displayed **Import and Export Wizard** dialog box, under **Choose an action to perform**, click **Import from another program or file**, and then click **Next**. In the **Import a File** dialog box, under **Select file type to import from**, click **Outlook Data File (.pst)**, and then click **Next**.

3 In the **Import Outlook Data File** dialog box, click **Browse**. In the **Open Outlook Data Files** dialog box, navigate to the location where the student files for this textbook are stored. Locate the file **o01D_Job_Fair_Contacts**, click it one time to select it, and then click **Open**. In the **Import Outlook Data File** dialog box, click **Next**, and then click **Finish**.

4 On the **Navigation Bar**, click the **People** button. In the **Folder Pane**, be sure your **Contacts** folder is displayed. Notice that the folder contains six contact records.

5 On the **Home tab**, in the **New group**, click **New Contact**, and then create a new contact record as follows:

Name:	**Jason Moran**
Company:	**Park Associates Network Solutions, Inc.**
Email address:	**JMoran@parkassociates.com**
Business phone:	**(626) 555-0134**
Business address:	**333 Rio Grande Ave**
	Desert Park, AZ 95123

6 On the **Contact tab** of the contact form ribbon, in the **Actions group**, click **Save & Close**.

7 Open the contact form for **Laura Wilson-Chavez**, change her **Work** phone number to **(805) 555-0159** Click **Save**, and then **Close** the form.

8 Click the **File tab**, click **Print**, and then under **Settings**, click **Phone Directory Style**. Under **Printer**, click **Print Options**. In the **Print** dialog box, click **Page Setup**.

9 In the **Page Setup: Phone Directory Style** dialog box, click the **Format tab**. Under **Options**, clear the **Headings for each letter** check box. Click the **Paper tab**. Under **Orientation**, click **Portrait** if this option is not already selected. Then click **OK**.

10 At the bottom of the **Print** dialog box, click **Preview**. In the lower right corner of the print preview, click the **Actual Size** button.

11 Start **PowerPoint 2016** and click **Blank Presentation**. On the **Home tab**, in the **Slides** group, click **Layout**, and then in the displayed gallery, click **Blank**.

12 With Slide 1 displayed in PowerPoint, on the **Insert tab**, in the **Images group**, click **Screenshot**, and then under **Available Windows**, click the image of your Outlook window to insert it on the slide.

13 In PowerPoint, click the **File tab**, click **Save As**, and then click **Browse**. In the displayed **Save As** dialog box, if necessary, navigate to your **Outlook Chapter 1** folder and open it. Click in the **File name** box, and then, using your own name, replace the selected text by typing **Lastname_Firstname_1D_Outlook** Click **Save**, and then **Minimize** ▬ the PowerPoint window.

(Project 1D Contacts, Tasks, and Appointments continues on the next page)

14 On the **Print** page, click the **Back** button to return to the **People** module without printing the phone directory.

15 On the **Navigation Bar**, click the **Tasks** button. Create the following tasks by clicking **New Task**, in the **New group**. Be sure to save and close each task form as you create it.

- Create a task with the subject **Finalize exhibitor list** Set the **Due Date** to two business days from today's date. Set the **Priority** to **Low**.

- Create a task with the subject **Contact rental company regarding setup** Set the **Due Date** to three weeks from today.

- Create a task with the subject **Write press release for job fair** Set the **Due Date** to tomorrow. Set the **Priority** to **High**.

16 In the list of three tasks, if necessary click the task regarding the press release to display it in the **Reading Pane** on the right. From the Windows taskbar, open your **Lastname_Firstname_1D_Outlook** presentation, and create a new blank slide. With Slide 2 displayed in PowerPoint, on the **Insert tab**, in the **Images group**, click **Screenshot**, and then under **Available Windows**, click the image of your Outlook window to insert it on the slide. Then **Save** 🖫 your presentation, and **Minimize** − the PowerPoint window.

17 Click the **File tab**, and then click **Print**. Under **Settings**, click **Table Style**. Under **Printer**, click **Print Options**. In the **Print** dialog box, under **Print style**, click **Page Setup**. In the **Page Setup: Table Style** dialog box, click the **Header/Footer tab**. Delete any existing information from the header and footer boxes.

18 In the **Page Setup: Table Style** dialog box, click the **Paper tab**. Under **Orientation**, click **Portrait** if this option button is not already selected. Click **OK**, then at the bottom of the **Print** dialog box, click **Preview**.

19 On the **Print** page, click the **Back** button to return to the **Tasks** module without printing your To-Do List.

20 On the **Navigation Bar**, click **Calendar**. On the ribbon, click the **Folder tab**. In the **New group**, click **New Calendar**. In the displayed **Create New Folder** dialog box, in the **Name** box, type **Personal Calendar** and then click **OK**.

21 In the **Folder Pane**, under **My Calendars**, select the **Personal Calendar** check box and clear the **Calendar** check box to display only the Personal Calendar.

22 In the **Date Navigator**, to the right of the month name, click the **right arrow** one time to advance the calendar to the next month. Click the **Monday** of the first full week of the displayed month. On the **View tab**, set the **Arrangement** to **Week**. Then click the **Home tab**. In the displayed week, create the following appointments by clicking **New Appointment** in the **New group**. Be sure to save and close the appointment forms as you create them.

- Monday:
  - As the **Subject**, type **Meet with Bradley to discuss Job Fair refreshments**
  - As the **Location**, type **Bradley's office**
  - Set the **Start time** to **10:00 AM** and **End time** to **11:00 AM**.

(Project 1D Contacts, Tasks, and Appointments continues on the next page)

- Tuesday:
  - As the **Subject**, type **Meet with Jane Houston**
  - As the **Location**, type **My office**
  - Set the **Start time** to **1:00 PM** and **End time** to **1:30 PM**.
  - Set the **Reminder** time to **30 minutes**.
- Thursday:
  - As the **Subject**, type **Pre-Fair Staff Meeting**
  - As the **Location**, type **West Conference Room**
  - Set the **Start time** to **9:00 AM** and the **End time** to **11:00 AM**.

23 From the Windows taskbar, display your **Lastname_Firstname_1D_Outlook** presentation, and create a new slide in the blank layout. With Slide 3 displayed in PowerPoint, on the **Insert tab**, in the **Images group**, click **Screenshot**, and then under **Available Windows**, click the image of your Outlook window to insert it on the slide.

24 **Save** 🖫 your presentation, and **Close** ☒ the PowerPoint window.

25 Click the **File tab**, click **Print**, and then under **Settings**, click **Weekly Agenda Style**. Under **Printer**, click **Print Options**. In the **Print** dialog box, under **Print style**, click **Page Setup**.

26 In the **Page Setup: Weekly Agenda Style** dialog box, click the **Paper tab**. Under **Orientation**, click **Portrait** if this option button is not already selected. Click **OK**. At the bottom of the **Print** dialog box, click **Preview**. Then on the **Print** page, click the **Back** button to return to the **Calendar** module without printing the weekly agenda.

27 In the **Folder Pane**, right-click **Personal Calendar**, and then on the displayed shortcut menu, click **Delete Calendar**. When the message *Move "Personal Calendar" to your Deleted Items folder* displays, click **Yes**.

28 On the **Navigation Bar**, click the **People** button. Press ⌨Ctrl + ⌨A to select all the Contacts, and then press ⌨Delete. On the **Navigation Bar**, click the **Tasks** button, press ⌨Ctrl + ⌨A to select all tasks, press ⌨Delete, and then click **OK**. On the **Navigation Bar**, click the **Mail** button. In the **Folder Pane**, right-click the **Deleted Items** folder, click **Empty Folder,** and then click **Yes**.

29 **Close** Outlook. Submit your **Lastname_Firstname_1D_Outlook** PowerPoint presentation to your instructor as directed.

> **END | You have completed Project 1D**

RUBRIC

The following outcomes-based assessments are *open-ended assessments*. That is, there is no specific correct result; your result will depend on your approach to the information provided. Make *Professional Quality* your goal. Use the following scoring rubric to guide you in *how* to approach the problem, and then to evaluate *how well* your approach solves the problem.

The *criteria*—Software Mastery, Content, Format and Layout, and Process—represent the knowledge and skills you have gained that you can apply to solving the problem. The *levels of performance*—Professional Quality, Approaching Professional Quality, or Needs Quality Improvements—help you and your instructor evaluate your result.

	Your completed project is of Professional Quality if you:	Your completed project is Approaching Professional Quality if you:	Your completed project Needs Quality Improvements if you:
1-Software Mastery	Choose and apply the most appropriate skills, tools, and features and identify efficient methods to solve the problem.	Choose and apply some appropriate skills, tools, and features, but not in the most efficient manner.	Choose inappropriate skills, tools, or features, or are inefficient in solving the problem.
2-Content	Construct a solution that is clear and well organized, contains content that is accurate, appropriate to the audience and purpose, and is complete. Provide a solution that contains no errors of spelling, grammar, or style.	Construct a solution in which some components are unclear, poorly organized, inconsistent, or incomplete. Misjudge the needs of the audience. Have some errors in spelling, grammar, or style, but the errors do not detract from comprehension.	Construct a solution that is unclear, incomplete, or poorly organized, containing some inaccurate or inappropriate content, and contains many errors of spelling, grammar, or style. Do not solve the problem.
3-Format and Layout	Format and arrange all elements to communicate information and ideas, clarify function, illustrate relationships, and indicate relative importance.	Apply appropriate format and layout features to some elements, but not others. Overuse features, causing minor distraction.	Apply format and layout that does not communicate information or ideas clearly. Do not use format and layout features to clarify function, illustrate relationships, or indicate relative importance. Use available features excessively, causing distraction.
4-Process	Use an organized approach that integrates planning, development, self-assessment, revision, and reflection.	Demonstrate an organized approach in some areas, but not others; or, use an insufficient process of organization throughout.	Do not use an organized approach to solve the problem.

Go! Think   Project 1E Child Center

 PROJECT FILES

For Project 1E, you will need the following file:

New email message form

You will save your results in a PowerPoint file as:

Lastname_Firstname_1E_Child_Center

Lake Michigan City College operates a fully staffed child development center for use by its students, faculty, and staff. Because of the college's large adult education program, the center is an important resource for students. The child development center falls under the control of Clarence Krasnow, Director of Resource Development. Dr. James Smith, Vice President of Student Affairs, is creating an information sheet about the child development center that will be included in the student packet for incoming adult students.

Compose an email message from Mr. Krasnow to Dr. Smith, in which you describe the facility, staff, and hours of operation of the center.

From the Outlook profile you are using for this textbook, start Outlook and maximize the screen. Compose a new email message to James Smith, whose email address is JSmith@LakeMichCityCollege.edu. Type a subject for the message that defines the purpose of the message, which is a description of the child development center.

For the text of the message, write three paragraphs of general information—an introductory paragraph describing the facility, a second paragraph describing the staff, and a third paragraph that covers the hours of operation. Suggestion: To help you compose your paragraphs, visit the website of your college to see whether it has a child development center or go to www.pasadena.edu/cdc.

Close the message using the name Clarence, and change the message importance to High.

With your message displayed on the screen, open PowerPoint, create a new presentation using the Blank slide layout, and then insert a screenshot of the Outlook window on the first slide. Using your own name, save your presentation in your **Outlook Chapter 1** folder as **Lastname_Firstname_1E_Child_Center** Submit your PowerPoint presentation to your instructor as directed.

Close the email message and then close Outlook without saving any changes.

END | You have completed Project 1E

Go! Think   Project 1F Athletic Center

 PROJECT FILES

For Project 1F, you will need the following file:

New email message form

You will save your results in a PowerPoint file as:

Lastname_Firstname_1F_Athletic_Center

Dr. James Smith, Vice President of Student Affairs at Lake Michigan City College, is preparing a brochure for incoming students that describes the college's athletic facilities. The college has recently received a very large donation from an alumnus for a new athletic center. Darron Jacobsen is responsible for facilities management. Dr. Smith has asked Mr. Jacobsen for a brief summary of the new facility. Construction has not yet begun, and the facility has yet to be named. It is expected that it will bear the name of the donor. Compose an email message from Darron Jacobsen to James Smith describing the features of the new facility.

From the Outlook profile you are using for this textbook, start Outlook and maximize the screen. Compose a new email message to James Smith, whose email address is JSmith@LakeMichCityCollege.edu. Type a subject for the message that defines the purpose of the message, which is a description of the new athletic center.

For the text of the message, type three paragraphs—an introductory paragraph describing the facility, a second paragraph describing the expected start and completion dates of construction, and a third paragraph that discusses how the college has not made a decision yet on the name of the facility. Suggestion: Conduct an Internet search using www.google.com and the search term **construction + "athletic center"** to find some information for your paragraphs.

Close the message using the name Darron, and change the message importance to High.

With your message displayed on the screen, open PowerPoint, create a new presentation using the Blank slide layout, and then insert a screenshot of the Outlook window on the first slide. Using your own name, save your presentation in your **Outlook Chapter 1** folder as **Lastname_Firstname_1F_Athletic_Center** Submit your PowerPoint presentation to your instructor as directed.

Close the email message and then close Outlook without saving any changes.

END | You have completed Project 1F

Index

Microsoft account, 3
Month arrangement, 50

N

Navigation Bar, 9
Notes area, 41

O

Offline, 12
Online, 12
Outcomes-based assessments, 70–72
Outlook
    configuring, for sending and receiving messages, 12–13
    configuring, to connect to email account, 6–10
    default settings, 36–38
    free email account, creation of, 55–57
    functions of, 2
    help, 36–38
    screen elements, 9
Outlook Help, 36–38
Outlook Today (screen), 8

P

Peek, 49
People Card, 40
People module, 10–11
    importing contact records into, 40–41
Personal Information Manager, 3
Print style, 33
Printing, email messages, 33–35

Q

Quick Access Toolbar, 9

R

RE: (prefix), 21
Reading Pane, 9
Ribbon, 9
Ribbon Display Options, 9
Ribbon group, 9
Ribbon tab, 9

S

Selecting text, 23
Sensitivity (of email message), 24
Sorting, email messages, 29–32
Spelling checker, 27–28
Status bar, 9
Syntax, email address, 14

T

Table Style (printing), 33
Tasks, 3, 47
    managing, 47–49
    project, 66–69
Tasks module, 11
Tell Me box, 9
Text, email messages
    formatting, 24–27
    selecting, 23
Title bar, 9
To-Do List
    creating and printing, 47–49

U

User account, 4

V

Views, 3

W

Week arrangement, 50
Windows
    mail profile in, creation of, 3–6
Windows Mail app, 55–57
Wizard, 16
Work Week arrangement, 50

Z

Zoom button, 9
Zoom slider, 9